To my Family—with much love and respect

My Parents—Alfred and Maud Murch
Michael and Jeanne Murch
Wendy and Michael Crowley
Trevor Murch

*who prepared me for managing the greatest and
most challenging project of all:*

–Life–

Project Management

Best Practices for IT Professionals

Richard Murch

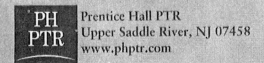

Prentice Hall PTR
Upper Saddle River, NJ 07458
www.phptr.com

Library of Congress Cataloging-in-Publication Data

Murch, Richard.
  Project management / Richard Murch
    p. cm. -- (Harris Kern's Enterprise computing institute)
  ISBN 0-13-021914-2
  1. Industrial project management. I. Title. II. Series.

HD69.P75 M865 2001
658.5--dc21

                                        00-056664

Editorial/production supervision: *Vincent Janoski*
Acquisitions editor: *Greg Doench*
Editorial Assistant: *Mary Treacy*
Marketing manager: *Bryan Gambrel*
Manufacturing manager: *Alexis Heydt*
Cover design director: *Jerry Votta*

Published by Prentice Hall PTR
Prentice-Hall, Inc.
Upper Saddle River, NJ 07458

Prentice Hall books are widely used by corporations and government agencies
for training, marketing, and resale.

The publisher offers discounts on this book when ordered in bulk quantities.
For more information, contact: Corporate Sales Department, Phone: 800-382-3419;
Fax: 201-236-7141; E-mail: corpsales@prenhall.com; or write: Prentice Hall PTR,
Corp. Sales Dept., One Lake Street, Upper Saddle River, NJ 07458.

Printed in the United States of America

    13 14 15 16 17 18 19   BKM BKM   0 9 8 7 6 5 4

ISBN 0-13-021914-2

Prentice-Hall International (UK) Limited, *London*
Prentice-Hall of Australia Pty. Limited, *Sydney*
Prentice-Hall Canada Inc., *Toronto*
Prentice-Hall Hispanoamericana, S.A., *Mexico*
Prentice-Hall of India Private Limited, *New Delhi*
Prentice-Hall of Japan, Inc., *Tokyo*
Pearson Education Asia Pte. Ltd.
Editora Prentice-Hall do Brasil, Ltda., *Rio de Janeiro*

Contents

v

Chapter 4

Project Teams   43

Part 3

The Project Management Lifecycle   55

Chapter 5

▶ Project Lifecycle Overview   57

Chapter 6

Project Planning Phase 69

Chapter 7

Analysis and Design Phases 79

Chapter 8

Construction Phase   99

Chapter 10

Roll-out Planning and Implementation Phase   125

Part 4

Project Management Techniques

Chapter 11

Project Management Methodologies

Chapter 12

Managing Rapid Application Development 147

Chapter 15

Other Techniques   187

Part 5

Special Topics in Project Management   201

Chapter 16

Knowledge Management   203

Chapter 17

Project Management and the Internet   211

Appendix A

Software Engineering Institute   221

Preface

Project management leadership has become a highly sought-after skill. An increasingly competitive global marketplace demands that businesses get new products, services, and business development completed quickly, on time, and within budget.

From small companies to web-based businesses to giant global financial institutions, project managers are fueling much of the successful development of exciting new business enterprises. They do this by delivering projects that have consistent value and help increase profits.

Talented and knowledgeable project managers will command the best assignments, salaries, other compensation and bonuses. They are the future business leaders, entrepreneurs, and global citizens, proving their value to any organization competing in today's fast-paced marketplace.

Regardless of how much in demand they are, good project managers are not born, but rather created through a combination of experience, time, talent, and training. Although excellent organizational skills are a prerequisite for the project manager, other key attributes may not be naturally occurring and need to be developed. Unfortunately, most of this development time occurs on the job, so few individuals who are promoted to the role of project manager ever feel fully ready to take on the challenge offered to them.

When faced with a first project, many project managers are worried that they don't yet know what they should know. Historically, project management, particularly in the Information Technology (IT) arena, has had a reputation for always being late and over budget. Even under the best of circumstances, project management is not easy; the project manager is continually faced with changing conditions, technology, resources, requirements, and schedules. Technology only serves to complicate matters further because today's computing environments tend to become obsolete with ever-increasing speed. Thus, a good project manager must not only be proficient at managing, but he or she must retain that proficiency as the technology changes. This light-speed adaptability is not an option, but rather an absolute requirement of the job. Clearly, the job of project manager is not for the faint-of-heart. Good preparation and knowledge about what the job entails is hugely valuable and key to surviving a first project.

The purpose of this book is to provide the new project manager with an accessible resource that presents the key topics and subject areas that he or she is likely to encounter. The book's broad coverage should be especially useful to a busy project manager who will not have time initially to research all of these topics in-depth but requires an immediate working knowledge of the overall functions and behaviors of an IT project. As the project manager becomes more comfortable with the basics, the book continues to be a valuable tool because it includes a wealth of additional resources such as books, papers, and web sites for additional learning as needed.

The hardest part of any project is knowing where to begin. It is hoped that this book will be a great jumping-off point to a successful career of well-managed endeavors for many a project manager.

▶ Who Should Read this Book

This book is intended for the novice project manager responsible for IT projects, regardless of size or complexity. Because of the broad nature of its coverage, it can be used as an introduction to key topics on the entire project lifecycle for someone previously unfamiliar with the nature of IT projects. For moderately experienced individuals, it can become a convenient reference manual to help reinforce the basic understanding of IT project management. Additionally, the sections on specialized topics will be useful to project managers seeking to increase their learning and to grow their experience base into niche areas such as Knowledge Management or Risk and Crisis Management.

▶ Organization of this Book

This book is organized into five parts that broadly categorize the information contained in it. These parts and their subjects are:

Part One: Introduction to Project Management provides a brief overview of this book and some historical background on Project Management and its overall evolution.

Part Two: Principles of Project Management covers ground-floor information such as basic skills, elements of project planning and reporting, and the makeup and issues surrounding good project teams.

Part Three: The Project Management Lifecycle categorizes the project by phase, explains each phase's purpose and describes in finer detail the activities, deliverables, and resources for and intentions of each phase.

Part Four: Project Management Techniques provides information on a number of techniques and topics facing Project Managers today, such as the types and use of methodologies, managing risks and problems, and specializations such as Software Quality Assurance, Configuration Management, and Crisis Management.

Part Five: Special Topics in Project Management concludes the main portion of this book with some discussion of hot topics such as Knowledge Management and the impact of the Internet on Project Management.

Finally, there are numerous additional sources of information available to the Project Manager included in several Appendices.

Part 1

Introduction to Project Management

Evolution of Project Management

How often your Re-volution has proven but E-volution
Alfred Lord Tennyson
poet (1809–1892)

▶ Introduction

Today, project managers play a key role in launching new products and managing for success. As leaders in the IT industry, project managers create strategies and orchestrate carefully designed action plans to complete projects successfully, often incorporating complex, dynamic and changing requirements. *Fortune* magazine calls it *Career Number 1*, and project management is becoming a top career choice for many highly talented professionals. What can be more satisfying than managing and delivering a project that creates value and profit?

We owe the success of modern project management practices to many previous events, people, and history over the course of hundreds of years. We could express the view that the very earliest examples of managing projects could go back as far as the cave dwellers. They had to set about finding and locating the very basic fundamentals, such as food, heat and shelter. This was managing to achieve objectives—in this case, survival.

Who actually invented the original term *project management* is now lost in the mists of history. There have been significant milestones that have advanced the development of modern project management, and it is helpful to understand the relationships and how they evolved.

▶ Industrial Revolution

The earliest forms of modern project management can be found during the Industrial Revolution. The roots of the Industrial Revolution began in the author's native United Kingdom in the late eighteenth century. At that time, the United Kingdom was the most powerful nation on Earth, almost equivalent to the United States today. It ruled empires and had the political strength and all of the components necessary to sustain a revolution of such magnitude that it would change the face of the planet for all time. It had wealth, entrepreneurs, and financial markets to promote new automation, factories, and manufacturing and management techniques. After its start in the United Kingdom, the revolution quickly spread, first to France and Germany, then eventually to the United States.

It was a time of great innovation and lasted for a period of about 150 years. Major advances in technology occurred during this time, such as:

- Cement was invented by John Smeaton, an Englishman, in 1756.
- The steam engine was invented by James Watt in 1770.
- The spinning jenny used in textile manufacturing was invented by James Hargreaves in 1764.
- The railway locomotive was invented by George Stephenson in 1814.
- The Bessemer steel process was invented by Henry Bessemer in 1856.
- The electric furnace was invented by William Siemens in 1861.

The Industrial Revolution brought the power of machines—before this time, only primitive machines were used to manufacture goods and services. The energy or power they used came entirely from sweat or muscle. When the power of machines became evident, it spawned the concept of factories and mass production that ushered in the revolution. Advances in steam power, together with new technologies of coal production, petroleum refining, and others, contributed to this revolution. The introduction of the telegraph as a communication technology added the final component to the revolution.

There was a social price to pay in terms of human exploitation. Children and women laborers often worked in appalling conditions. The reforms of organizations, such as the Chartist Movement, a moral force that demanded change through peaceful methods of persuasion and other reformers, would work hard and long to abolish these intolerable working conditions.

▶ Key People in Early Project Management

Frederick Taylor (1856–1915) was an American industrialist and an early pioneer of management techniques. On his gravestone in Pennsylvania is inscribed the epitaph the "Father of Management." He used a scientific approach to understanding the steps in completing a product and using money to create added incentive for workers who exceed the "average" level of production. He spent some time studying the basic work principles in steel mills and developed his management principle from them.

In 1911, Taylor published a landmark book, *Principles of Scientific Management*, in which he proposed work methods designed to increase worker productivity significantly. Although many organizations adopted his methods at that time, organized labor unions in the United States strongly objected to Taylor's proposals, which led to a good deal of controversy and Congressional hearings.

The Taylor Model is an important milestone in the evolution of management theory. Before this, the only way to obtain productivity increases was to demand more workers or to get people to work longer and harder. Taylor's principles gave rise to dramatic productivity increases. He was the first person to encourage management and employees to "work smarter."

Taylor's management principles included:

- Analyze each job to specify optimal procedures

- Match skills with tasks to be accomplished
- Understand worker characteristics that are important for increased productivity
- Train workers to be more productive
- Set a "fair day's work" standard for productivity expectations
- Document worker performance
- Reward performance with incentives and bonuses
- Complete management and reporting of all work

An associate of Frederick Taylor was Henry Gantt (1861–1919). He became famous for the Gantt chart that we use today in project management. Gantt studied the construction of U.S. Navy ships during World War I and found that he could understand the complexities of construction much better by drawing charts. An example of this kind of chart appears in Figure 1–1, below.

Gantt invented techniques such as milestone deliverables, task duration, and estimates. Although enhanced with modern techniques such as dependencies, much of the content and format of Gantt charts has remained unchanged for 100 years. This is a remarkable

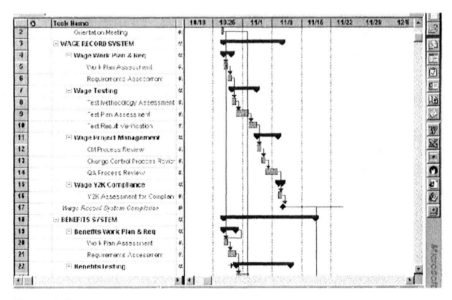

Figure 1–1   Example of a Gantt chart.

feat of technology endurance, particularly in an age that justifies changes in terms of minutes.

Henry Gantt began project management by asking some fundamental questions, then expressing them in a graphical format. He asked questions such as:

- How long will the project take?
- What are the critical tasks that must be completed?
- How long will each task take?
- When must each task start and end?
- Who will be responsible for each task?
- What resources will be required to complete each task?
- How will delayed tasks affect the project?
- What is the impact of a modification to the project scope?
- What is the total cost of the project?
- What is the cost of each task?
- Is the project on schedule?
- How can slippage problems be corrected?
- What is the project's cost at any point in time?
- Is there a way to speed up the project?

Another significant pioneer at this time was Dr. W. Edwards Deming (1900–1993). Just as Frederick Taylor was the father of management, so we can claim Deming as the father of quality. Born in 1900, he grew up on a Wyoming homestead just as the new frontier was taming the Wild West. During World War II, he taught courses throughout the country. His emphasis on quality in the United States led to the creation of the American Society of Quality Control, of which Deming was a charter member. Immediately after the war, his services were in demand overseas, and it was then that he first visited Japan. The term *made in Japan* was about to take on an entirely new meaning as it became known as the Japanese miracle. Meanwhile, the management techniques developed by Frederick Taylor were gaining wide acceptance in post-war America.

Deming realized that management was wrong to be committed to quotas and punishing for mistakes, and that it would have to have visionary leaders to achieve quality. From that need, Deming created his now-famous 14 Points to provide a management theory to support his ideas, and the rest is history. Figure 1–2 illustrates Deming as we know him.

Basic Deming management philosophy is summarized below:

1. Create Constancy of Purpose for the Improvement of All Products and Services
2. Adopt New Management Philosophy
3. Cease Dependence on Mass Inspection
4. End the Practice of Awarding Business on Price Tag Alone
5. Improve Constantly and Forever the System of Production and Service
6. Establish Training and Retraining
7. Create Management Leadership
8. Drive Out Fear—Do Not Punish for Mistakes
9. Break Down Barriers Between Staff Areas
10. Eliminate Slogans, Exhortations, and Targets for the Work Force
11. Eliminate Numerical Quotas
12. Remove Barriers to Pride of Proficiency
13. Institute a Vigorous, Continuous Program of Education and Retraining
14. Take Action To Accomplish the Transformation

For over 40 years after the end of World War II, Deming continued his work, evolving theories, writing books, consulting with governments

Figure 1–2   Dr. W. Edwards Deming. His aim was to foster the advancement of commerce, prosperity, and peace.

and industry, conducting seminars, and making improvements in managing for quality. Managing projects the Deming way has had a profound effect on the overall quality of projects.

▶ Other Significant Events

Many other events and people have contributed to the modern success of project management. This book has attempted to list some of the more significant milestones, beginning from the Industrial Revolution.

World War I	The mobilization of manufacturing of guns and ammunitions in large quantities. Development of tanks, flight, and other technology.
1920s–1930	Peace and working toward creating better output, better productivity, and mass production. Henry Ford's Model T is a case in point.
World War II	War again meant building better, faster ships, and planes, and moving people to fight in remote parts of the world. Radar, jet engines, and other technologies invented. First computers appeared.
1950s	The nuclear age is ushered in with terrible weapons. During this time, a great number of inventions in electronics, health, and manufacturing appeared.
The Space Age	The Space Age brings huge advances in computers, communications, and many other technologies. First computers with transistors appeared in 1954.
Mainframes	In mid-1960, IBM launches Project 360, developed by Gene Amdahl. A mainframe computer, the IBM 360 series, had interchangeable peripherals and devices. Mainframes had arrived.

The Silicon Chip	The microprocessor comes into its own with an increasing number of transistors on a single wafer. Geoffrey Moore postulates his law of doubling transistors on chips.
4GLs	Work on advances such as Fourth-Generation Languages (4GLs) appear. In 1982 and 1983, the author researched a book for James Martin—*Application Development without Programmers*—which suggests that we can develop and manage projects much better if we use end users and new software.

▶ Conclusions

Project management is a continuing set of process improvement initiatives. We have gained much in a short space of time. From the Industrial Revolution and improvements in delivering goods and services to the early days of the 1950s, when project management software ran on mainframes, to the sophisticated software of today that can show managers instantly where they are in a project. Although the tools and the methods may have changed and continue to evolve, the key components of project management remain constant. It is about people, processes, and technology working together in a powerful union to do things better, faster, and more efficiently.

Part 2

Principles of
Project Management

Basic Skills for Project Managers

Be not afraid of greatness; some are born great; some achieve greatness—others have greatness thrust upon them.

William Shakespeare
Twelfth Night

▶ Introduction

Before now, we had discussed project management in the broad sense, that is, from the perspective that any type of project—industrial assembly line, new construction, or technology implementation—operated by the same sets of rules and processes. For the remainder of this book, we focus on the last type of project and its leader—the IT project manager.

Project managers are a very special breed of people. They are in much demand and will be increasingly so as the need for effective technologists continues to soar. Good technology project managers are trained, not born. They develop skills through experience and education. They become better project managers each time they successfully deliver a project. They learn new techniques and apply them on their projects. They learn lessons—sometimes the hard way—to be better managers in the future.

13

▶ What Does a Project Manager Do?

Briefly, technology project managers fulfill the following broad requirements:

- Define and review the business case and requirements by regular reviews and controls to ensure that the client receives the system that he or she wants and needs.
- Initiate and plan the project by establishing its format, direction, and base lines that allow for any variance measurements and change control.
- Partner with the end users, work with project sponsors and other management to establish progress and direction of the project by achieving goals, reaching targets, solving problems, mitigating risks.
- Manage the technology, people, and change in order to achieve goals, reach targets, and deliver the project on time and within budget.
- Manage the project staff by creating an environment conducive to the delivery of the new application in the most cost-effective manner.
- Be able to manage uncertainty, rapid change, ambiguity, surprises, and a less defined environment.
- Manage the client relationship by using an adequate direct yet complete and formal reporting format that compliments a respected and productive relationship.
- Drive the project by leading by example, and motivating all-concerned until the project accomplishes its goal.

Now let us examine the skills and qualities needed to meet these requirements.

▶ Necessary Skills

The skills that a good project manager possesses are many and varied, covering the entire spectrum of the human personality. We can divide these skills into a number of specific categories, namely:

Personal Skills

Project Managers must be able to motivate and sustain people. Project team members will look to the project manager to solve problems and help with removing obstacles. Project managers must be able to address and solve problems within the team, as well as those that occur outside the team. There are numerous ways, both subtle and direct, in which project managers can help team members.

Some examples include the following:

- Manage by example (MBE). Team members will be closely watching all actions of the project manager. Therefore, project managers must be honest, direct, straightforward, and knowledgeable in all dealings with people and with the project. A good manager knows how to work hard and have fun, and this approach becomes contagious.

- A positive attitude. Project managers must always have a positive attitude, even when there are substantial difficulties, problems, or project obstacles. Negative attitudes erode confidence, and a downward spiral will follow.

- Define expectations. Managers who manage must clearly define what is expected of team members. It is important to do this in writing—get agreement from the individual team members. This leaves no room for problems later, when someone states "It's not my job." Performance expectations *must* be defined at the start of the project.

- Be considerate. Project management is a demanding job with a need for multiple skills at many levels. Above all, be considerate and respectful, and give people and team members the time and consideration they deserve. Make people aware that their efforts are appreciated and the work that they do is important, because it is. A letter, personal word, or e-mail of appreciation goes a long way.

- Be direct. Project managers are respected if they are direct, open, and deal with all types of problems. Never conceal problems or avoid addressing them. If a problem is bigger than the project manager or the team can deal with, escalate it to senior management. Never make commitments that cannot be delivered.

- Finally, a favorite and personal rule of the author: "Under-promise, then over-deliver."

Technical Skills

There are two schools of thought about the level needed for technical skills. Some project managers prefer to have little technical knowledge about the projects they manage, preferring to leave the technical management to other junior managers, such as programming managers or network managers. Others have detailed technical skills of computer languages, software, and networks.

There is no hard and fast rule. It really depends on the type and size of projects, their structure, resources available, and the project environment.

Questions that project managers should ask include the following:

1. What types of technical problems require management?
2. Who will solve them?
3. Is it done with quality and satisfaction?
4. Who can I rely on in my project team?
5. What outside resources, if any, can I draw on for assistance?

As with all employees, project managers should have the technical knowledge and skills needed to do their jobs. If managers lack these skills, training is one option; being mentored or coached by a more experienced individual is another. Senior management should ask the question, Do your project managers need more technical skills than they already possess?

On larger complex projects, such as systems integration projects or multiple-year projects, there are frequently too many complex technologies for the project manager to master. Technical training that provides breadth may be useful. On smaller projects, the project manager may also be a key technical contributor. In this case, technical training may enhance the abilities of project managers to contribute technically, but it is unlikely to improve their management skills.

One thing is abundantly clear—the project manager is *ultimately* responsible for the entire management of the project, technical or otherwise, and will require solutions to the technical issues that will occur.

Management Skills

Project managers need other key skills besides those that are purely technical to lead and deliver on their projects successfully. A good project manager needs to understand many facets of the *business* aspect of running a project, so critical skills touch on expertise in the areas of organization, communication, finance, and human resources.

The following are examples of the management topics used in training effective project managers:

- Project planning, initiation, and organization
- Recruiting people and keeping them
- Effective project negotiation
- Software tools for project management
- Accurate estimating and cost control
- Project execution and control
- Developing powerful project presentations and reports
- Personal and project leadership
- Managing risk and making decisions
- Effective problem management
- Performance management
- Managing the projects within the organization
- Project management professional (PMP) exam review
- Growing and sustaining a high-performance team
- Managing change within an organization

This last skill cannot be over-emphasized. Although we worry about whether the technology selected is the correct one for the organization and will lead to success, projects do not generally fail because of lack of adequate technology. Statistically, most projects fail because the "soft science" portions of the project have not received enough attention—the human factor has not been adequately addressed. Change, whether for good or for bad, is stressful on an organization and its personnel. The ability to manage this change is one area in which any good project manager would do well to hone skills.

Coping Skills

A good project manager has to acquire a number of skills to cope with different situations, conflicts, uncertainty, and doubt. This means:

- Being flexible
- Being persistent and firm when necessary
- Being creative, even when the project does not call for it
- Absorbing large volumes of data from multiple sources
- Being patient but able to differentiate between patience and action
- Being able to handle large amounts of continuous, often unrelenting stress

Additionally, good project managers have high tolerance for surprises, uncertainty, and ambiguity. Projects rarely progress the way that they are defined, and managers need to manage the uncertainty that comes with that.

▶ Manage One Project—or Many?

There is no simple answer to this question: some managers are able to juggle multiple projects and disparate deadlines successfully, and others are not. In these days of multiple projects that have to be delivered quickly, it is very possible that management will require managing multiple projects. However, this brings a risk. Will project managers be stretched too thin? Again, there is no single, reliable answer. Project managers and senior management need to ask themselves some basic questions:

- How much support will be provided?
- How many people are on the project? Are they part-time or full-time?
- What are the management challenges? An adequately budgeted project may require less effort to manage than one that is extremely thin.

- Are all the projects in the same physical location or will the project manager spend a lot of time traveling?
- Do all the projects involve the same technology? The same business cultures? The same set of stakeholders?
- How many of the projects have important deadlines that are close together?

The answers to these questions will aid in determining whether multiple projects can share a management resource. The more complex the projects from the standpoints of staffing, budgeting, and technology, the more likely it is that they will need a dedicated resource to manage them adequately.

▶ Project Management Skills Development

One of the surest ways to align strategies and work force competencies with enterprise vision is to create a road map from vision to execution. A skills management process starts in the future and works its way back to the present. An IT skills management process, for example, links the enterprise vision to a technology forecast. The technology forecasts to required skills, the required skills to the IT skills inventory, the skills inventory to the IT staff's competence levels, and the competence levels to gaps and to the time frame during which those gaps need to be filled. Leadership, team building, marketing, business savvy, project management, manufacturing know-how, functional expertise, and institutional knowledge all are part of the skills picture.

Skills management serves as an order for managing the work force (see Figure 2–1). It lays out a road map for skills development, work role definition, career tracks, resource management, staffing allocation, workload balancing, and learning. With a road map, all members of the work force can fit their strengths, weaknesses, and alternatives into the enterprise's plans.

Skills management is becoming a lifeline in a turbulent IT labor market. Midsize and large enterprises, businesses in the private and public sectors, aggressive and conservative companies—all are looking at skills management with renewed interest. Many enterprises now recognize that the combined lack of enterprise planning, imagination, and

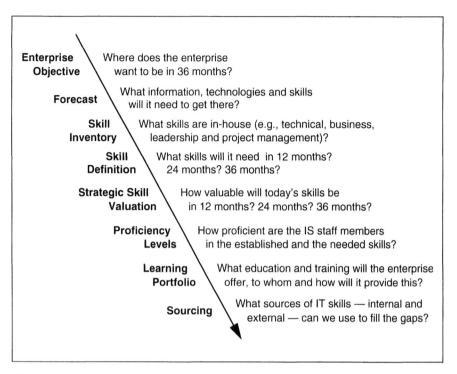

Enterprise
Objective   Where does the enterprise
want to be in 36 months?

Forecast   What information, technologies and skills
will it need to get there?

Skill
Inventory   What skills are in-house (e.g., technical, business,
leadership and project management)?

Skill
Definition   What skills will it need in 12 months?
24 months? 36 months?

Strategic Skill
Valuation   How valuable will today's skills be
in 12 months? 24 months? 36 months?

Proficiency
Levels   How proficient are the IS staff members
in the established and the needed skills?

Learning
Portfolio   What education and training will the enterprise
offer, to whom and how will it provide this?

Sourcing   What sources of IT skills — internal and
external — can we use to fill the gaps?

Figure 2–1   Skills Management—A Road Map for the Work Force
(Source: Gartner Group, Inc.).

foresight are as much to blame for today's labor crunch as is the shortage of relevant IT skills. In that climate, skills management can be a powerful tool for bringing discipline, rationale, and cross-pollination to an underused process. Even more enticing, many IT professionals, under the mantle of career "entrepreneurism," will throw in their lot with enterprises that have clearly committed to and funded skills management programs. Having a road map with which to guide career development is more meaningful than wandering until serendipity strikes.

Three years ago, when large organizations first began covering the area of skills management, it was a process reserved for the most progressive enterprises. By methodically and meticulously forecasting, classifying, analyzing, and taking inventory of skills, progressive enterprises could identify the urgency and volume of skills gaps, create focused training programs, and add some rational thinking to their sourcing strategies. Skills management continues to satisfy those needs, even fostering a niche market of consultants and software developers that are eager to bring order to IT Human Resource management.

Before moving on, it is beneficial to make sure that everybody is speaking the same language. In the Gartner Group's definition of perspective, skills management is *a robust and systematic approach to forecasting, identifying, cataloguing, evaluating, and analyzing the work force skills, competencies and gaps that enterprises face.* Although many programs and initiatives adopt the label *skills management,* most of them focus on skills inventory and fall short in analysis and forecasting. A well-designed skills management process injects a stronger dose of discipline, coordination, and planning into work force planning, strategic planning, professional training and development programs, resource allocation maneuvering, and risk analysis and assessment.

Enterprises can reap several lessons from skills management. Skills management works if it:

- Defines skills for roles
- Forces forward thinking
- Forces some documentation of what makes an IT professional especially proficient
- Strengthens the organization
- Leads to focused training, risk assessment, sourcing strategy, and resource allocation via gap identification
- Attracts high-level endorsement

Skills management does not work if it:

- Does not define work roles
- Lacks plans or incentive for refreshment
- Communicates its purpose poorly
- Provides differing language and terminology
- Force-fits skills and work roles to policies, rather than driving new frameworks

Skills Management Case Study

A North American manufacturing company set a goal to boost revenue by $300 million within three years. Key to the growth was a new way of dealing with information and IT. First, hoarding of information by divisions had to give way to enterprise ownership of information. Second, ubiquitous access to information required a managed and enterprise-wide migration to standards, interoperability, common platforms, and client/server technology. Finally, the vision of ubiquitous access depended on substantially upgrading the IT organization's skill base, supplementing and supplanting mainframe skills with skills associated with distributed processing and client/server application development.

The company embarked on an ambitious initiative designed to cultivate the technical skills and business understanding of the IT professionals. The initiative—notably, company-wide skill identification and continuous training—will help the company to raise its skills level and will give IT employees control of their professional development.

Elements of the IT professional development initiative included:

- Identifying eight areas of IT professional skills, technical skills being only one area (a detailed discussion on the eight areas identified follows this list)

- Assigning company values to skills for the near term, short term, and long term

- Evaluating employee competence levels within the eight areas of IT professional skills

- Providing continuous training in critical skills, both technical and non-technical

- Establishing an IT mentor program

- Supervisors providing performance planning and coaching

- Establishing team and peer feedback

- Flattening the IT organization from 18 to 5 titles

- Mapping skills and performance values to "salary zones" within the flatter organization

With the help of outside experts, IT executives identified more than 125 skills in eight areas of IT professional development. The eight areas of focus for IT professional development and a sampling of associated skills include:

- *Customer focus*—employee possesses knowledge of customers' business needs and expectations; delivers constructive qualitative feedback to customers, meets deadlines, and works with customers to set requirements and schedules

- *Technical skills*—employee possesses skills related to programming, computer-aided software engineering, desktop client services, enterprise infrastructure applications, technical software, and hardware support

- *Product or technology evaluation and expertise*—employee analyzes and compares products, makes sound recommendations within the company architecture, understands and recognizes limitations of technologies, can communicate the fundamentals of technology to others, and uses technical team resources to resolve or avoid technology-based problems

- *Business and application expertise*—employee possesses knowledge of business-specific applications, knows company's business and local operations, knows the broad application environments (e.g., order entry and accounting), and understands general concepts of business management

- *Project management*—employee handles projects of certain size and complexity, estimates project costs and schedules with a degree of accuracy, executes project to plan, manages multiple projects at once, builds teams and organizes team resources, and knows project management tools

- *Interpersonal skills*—employee performs as team member or team leader, contributes knowledge to the team and to the organization, and communicates effectively

- *Administrative skills*—employee has understanding of budgeting, interviewing, economics of the business, and salary and review process

- *Soft skills*—employee displays leadership, forward thinking, initiative, drive for education, and commitment to organizational structure and development.

Each skill receives a weighting factor based on its strategic significance to the company during the next 12 months, the next 12 to 24 months, and the next 24 to 60 months. A skill considered critical to the company earns a weight of 6; a skill with no value to the company earns a weight of 0. After the company skills are identified and their weights assigned, employee skills are crosschecked against the company skills and assigned a score based on the employee's competence level. Employee competence levels range from 6 to 1, that is, from mastery to basic understanding. (A competence score of zero is reserved for skills that are either not applicable or not possessed by the employee.) Employees then compare their competence scores with those they receive from their peers, team leaders, and supervisors.

To see the scoring mechanism in action, assume that the company assigns COBOL programming skills a weight of 4 for the next 12 months and a weight of 3 for the following 12 to 24 months. At the same time, an IT employee earns a score of 3 for average skills in COBOL programming. Given the framework, the value of those skills to the employee will be 12 during the next 12 months, but the value will decline to 9 during the next 12 to 24 months.

Continuous training is considered essential to the program's success. Here, the IT executives are seeking to develop an implicit promise between the company and the employees. The company promises to provide the resources and opportunities for training—time, funding, and identification and valuation of strategic skills—if the employees promise to use the training to bridge gaps in the company skills base and in their own skill levels. Armed with the company skills inventory and personal competence scores, employees who take the appropriate training will see their value to the company rise. Employees who choose to forgo appropriate training will see their value diminish.

On the plus side, the skills and training program has forced the company to view the IT organization in terms of skills and long-term corporate objectives, not simply in terms of head count. Moreover, employees have responded positively to a program that puts professional development in their hands. On the negative side, skills identification and buy-in from IT managers take so long that the initiative risks losing momentum.

Keys to a Successful Skills Management Endeavor

Three areas must be worked out for a skills management initiative to be successful:

1. Employees have to adopt the program as their own, rather than as a management dictate, including the employees assuming control of their own professional development

2. Supervisors have to surrender some control over employee development

3. Executives must ensure that employees use metrics as a tool for professional development, not as a weapon in cutthroat competition

As enterprises turn to technology to reach the next level of corporate performance, IT organizations should identify the skills they need to meet the corporate objectives. Through a program of skills identification, IT organizations can see the holes in their coverage, set priorities for projects, define which training is required, and determine which skills may need third-party coverage. A commitment to funding for training is essential.

Conclusions

Rarely has a professional field evolved as rapidly as project management. It is totally different from what it was even 10 years ago. The struggle to stay abreast of new and rapidly evolving technologies, to deal with accumulated development and maintenance backlogs, and to cope with people issues has become a treadmill race as software groups work hard just to stay in place. A key goal of disciplined project managers is to avoid the surprises that can occur when these surprises almost always lead to bad news: canceled projects, late delivery, cost overruns, dissatisfied customers, outsourcing, termination, and unemployment. Indeed, we need to develop management by surprise (MBS) as a project management technique!

As we have discussed in this chapter, project managers are a special breed of people. The skills that they develop are a cross between a diplomat, ballet dancer, and a Marine Corps drill sergeant—all while having the patience of Job. These skills will serve them well for future higher-level positions as Vice Presidents, Chief Information Officers (CIOs), and Chief Executive Officers (CEOs) of the corporations for which they work.

The culture of an organization is a critical success factor in its efforts to survive, improve, and flourish. A culture based on a commitment to project management and delivering quality projects and effective management differentiates a team that practices excellent project management from a flock of individual programmers doing their best to ship code.

Projects rarely fail—but people do.

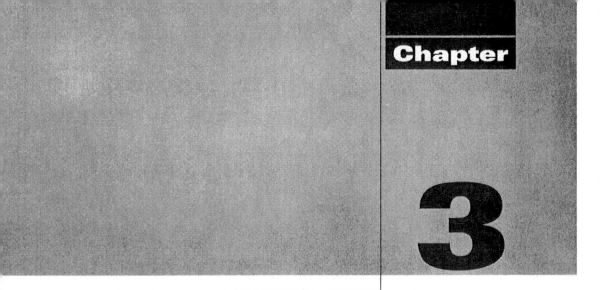

Project Planning and Reporting

If you plan for nothing—you will surely get there.
Anonymous

▶ Introduction

Being successful in project planning requires a detailed understanding of the project, discipline, and a methodology. Sound project plans are realistic, up-to-date, and reviewed frequently. Work is broken into manageable chunks, with extra time and budget allowed for contingencies. Users and the IT staff define what each stage will deliver and how the team will know when the project is complete. Project milestones enable the project board to make a "continue or stop" decision. Good plans enable project managers to identify problems early.

Here are some suggestions:

Define the Job in Detail. Determine exactly the mission of the project, what work must be done to deliver on the project vision, and what products must be delivered.

Get the Right People Involved. Involve the entire project team, including the customers, throughout the project, especially during early planning.

Estimate the Time and Costs.   Develop a detailed estimate of each phase of the development process before undertaking that phase.

Break the Job Down Using the XX Hour Rule.   Break the project down into deliverable products where XX equals no more than 10, 20, 30, 40 hours to complete.

Develop Project Standards.   Developing and agreeing on a basic set of project standards is key to delivering consistent, high-quality end products.

Establish a Change Procedure.   Recognize that change is an inherent and inevitable part of project lifecycle and plan for it.

Agree on Acceptance Criteria.   Determine in advance what will constitute an acceptable system.

▶ Project Planning Deliverables

Doomed projects have ill-specified deliverables. They talk about concepts rather than benefits. They concentrate on process—*how* the project will run—and forget the aims. In successful projects, users and the IT organizations both understand and agree on deliverables and benefits. Project managers who are able to learn lessons from their projects—successful or unsuccessful—achieve consistently better results. Executive sponsors should insist on regular "lessons learned" reviews during the project and following its implementation. These reviews are a good way of capturing new ideas and ways of working that will be valuable in the future.

The following is a list of deliverables that are generated during project planning:

- Project Organization Chart
- Project Milestones
- Confirmed Work Authorization—Statement of Work (SOW) or Project Charter
- Solution-Oriented Deliverables (i.e., copies of Solution Deliverables turned over to the Client or Program Management)
- Project Standards

- Project-Level Reports/Other Reports
  - Risk Reports
  - Quality Reports
  - Final Project Report
- Project Plan Documents
  - Work Plan, including Work Packages
  - Resource Plan
  - Project Schedule
  - Risk Mitigation Plan
  - Communication Plan
  - Testing Plan
  - Training Plan
  - Quality Plan
  - Project Management Plan
  - Implementation Plan
  - Acceptance Criteria for each Work Package
- Issue/Change Documents
  - Change Requests/Change Orders
  - Issue Assessments
  - Project Standards and Procedures
  - Project Correspondence

▶ Project Standards

The keys to successful projects are people, teamwork, and good standards, in that order. Project standards are agreed-upon documents that are used as guidelines in delivering the project. Standards help ensure that the work products are developed consistently by all team members, that they adhere to a common set of quality levels, and that they are communicated in a predictable and agreed-upon fashion. If companies adopt workable project management standards, it will make life easier for all concerned. What does not happen frequently enough is a review of standards. Project managers need to continually ask, How are we doing? Are we doing things the right way?

Most corporations today have a complete jumble of standards, if they have any at all. Frequently feuding business units adopt their own standards, often out of sheer belligerence and disagreement with corporate directives. It is a complex task that is not easily solved and is beyond the scope of this book. However, one clear directive should be apparent: At the project level, project managers should have a strong motive for improving the standards by which they manage their projects.

Table 3-1 represents a list of subject areas and deliverables where project managers should look to develop, upgrade, or improve their standards:

Table 3–1 Standards and Deliverables for the Project Manager

Project Management Standard Areas	Suggested Major Deliverables
Scope	Scope Document
	Project Charter
	Cost/Benefit Analysis
	Change Management Plan
	Configuration Management
	Requirements Management
Application Development	Module Specifications
	Programming Specifications
	Systems Development Plan
	Software Development Plan
	Release Management Plan
	Application Development Methodology
	Migration Strategy
Project Planning	Consolidated Project Budget
	Work Breakdown Structure (WBS)
	Earned Value Reports
	Project Costing Plan
	Configuration Management Plan
	Data Conversion Plan
	Project Status Report
Implementation	Test Plan
	Implementation Schedule Reports
	Project Implementation Estimate
	Release Management
Risk	Risk Management Plan
	Risk Response Document
	Business Continuity Plan

(continued)

Project Management Standard Areas	Suggested Major Deliverables
Communications	Project Communications Plan Issue Resolution Procedure
Human Resources	Resource Planning Process Internal/External Recruitment Plan Project Training Plans Conflict Resolution Procedure
Procurement	Outside Procurement Plan Requests for Proposals (RFPs) Subcontractor Management Plan
Quality	Software Quality Assurance Procedures Overall Quality Plan Quality Control Procedures Independent Verification and Validation Report—I V and V

If it can be justified in terms of resources and value, a separate Project Management Standards Unit could be staffed with sole responsibility of working to improve corporate-wide project management standards.

Valuable resources already exist on the Internet and with other institutions, such as the Project Management Institute (PMI), which has excellent, proven material that can be made available to the project. (See Appendix B.)

▶ How Much Detail?

Another key question with project planning is, How much detail should be put into the plan? The answer is not easy to explain. It really depends on the scope and duration of the project. On large complex projects with a budget of millions of dollars and hundreds of people working on it that runs for many months or years, you would expect to have detailed tasks, resource assignments, schedules, and budget controls. Smaller projects, with a small project team that will last for only a few weeks would have less detail and be managed to a higher level of tasks.

Skilled project managers develop a flair for having the right amount of detail to manage the project. If the level of detail is too high, more time will be spent managing the plan than managing the project. Another important issue to understand is that a plan should contain enough information to stand up to challenges or criticism.

▶ Project Status —An Example

One of the most important tasks a project manager can do regularly is to report the project's progress. This is no simple task and involves much detailed preparation, monitoring, and compiling of data. This data is presented to the project or executive sponsor or it might be presented to the project steering committee. The frequency of reporting can vary with project risk; for example, high-risk projects or projects that have problems may want to issue reports weekly.

As a general rule, it is good management practice to report progress monthly. What follows is an example of a project management status report, along with explanations for the types of information included. The author has used this template; it works for complex projects and reports all the relevant data, such as issues, risks, actions, costing, and projections.

Project Status Report

Reporting Month

Job Number (s)

Job Title

Customer

Contract Type

Period of Performance

Preparation Date
(due 10 days after month end)

Prepared by:
Signature, date

Project Manager
Signature, date

Software QA Manager
Signature, date

Table of Contents

Project Status

Project Cost Performance

Plan versus Actual

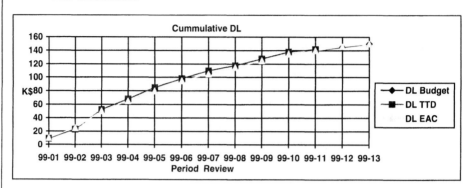

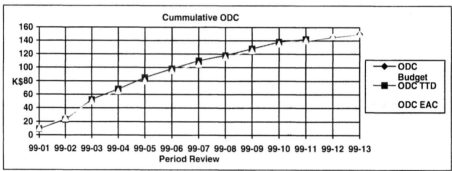

Plus Charts for Travel, Total Cost, and Profit

Analysis of Variance

Explain any significant variance (10% or greater) of actual to budget. Always explain any variance of EAC versus Budget.

Issues and Corrective Actions

Address cost issues, the proposed corrective action, and the status of the corrective action. Issues are carried forward on monthly status reports until the corrective action has corrected the issue.

Issues and Corrective Actions			
Issue ID	Issue	Corrective Action	Status of Corrective Action

Project Staffing Performance

Current versus Planned Staff
Using a chart or text to indicate staff requirements and plans for staffing, including roles, head count by role, and timing for head count.

Analysis of Variance.

Explain any variance

Staff Development (recruiting, training, etc.)

Issues and Corrective Actions

Issues and Corrective Actions			
Issue ID	Issue	Corrective Action	Status of Corrective Action

Project Schedule Performance

Current Versus Planned Schedule
Present a summary of the key project level activities, deliverables, and milestones. Present a high-level Gantt chart for the entire project and, if necessary, a detailed Gantt chart focusing on the next quarter's tasks.

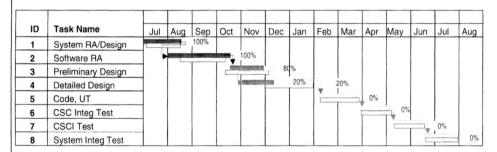

ID	Task Name	Jul	Aug	Sep	Oct	Nov	Dec	Jan	Feb	Mar	Apr	May	Jun	Jul	Aug
1	System RA/Design			100%											
2	Software RA					100%									
3	Preliminary Design						80%								
4	Detailed Design							20%		20%					
5	Code, UT										0%				
6	CSC Integ Test											0%			
7	CSCI Test													0%	
8	System Integ Test														0%

Analysis of Variance
Explain any schedule slippage that impacts a deliverable end date or impacts progress on other activities.

Accomplishments During Past Month—also reported to Customer

Plans for the Next Month—also reported to Customer

Issues and Corrective Actions

Issues and Corrective Actions (Y/N indicates whether reported to customer)				
Issue ID	Issue	Corrective Action	Status of Corrective Action	Y/N

Project Issues, Risks, Action Item Status

Conflicts and Issues Not Resolvable within the Project
Present issues not previously identified that need senior management attention for resolution.

Project Commitments and Changes to Commitments
Present any changes to commitments that senior management needs to be aware of, for example, if planned and committed personnel from another organization are not able to meet their obligations. This is important to manage outside risks.

Project Risks and Mitigation
Present a status of the major project risks, including those presented initially with the software development plan, as well as any new risks. A risk is defined as the possibility of suffering a loss. Risk management includes risk identification, assessment, analysis, control, and reporting. See Chapter 13 for more information on managing risks.

Project Risk Management				
Risk	Assessment	Risk Analysis	Mitigation Approach	Status of Mitigation Approach

Software Metrics

Actual versus Planned Size

Analysis of Variance

Issues and Corrective Actions

Issues and Corrective Actions			
Issue ID	Issue	Corrective Action	Status of Corrective Action

Project Software Quality Assurance (SQA) Activities And Results

Noncompliant Items

Noncompliant Items			
Total to Date	% Closed	% Open	Number Needing Senior Management Resolution
24	83%	17%	1

SQA Cost Performance

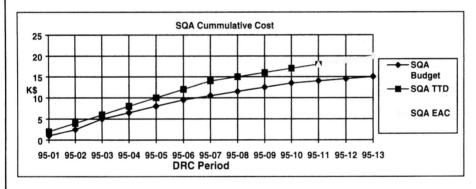

SQA Schedule

SQA Product and Activities Status			
PAL Item	Schedule	Actual	Comment
SDP Review			
Prepare SQAP			

Analysis of Variance

Issues and Corrective Actions

Issues and Corrective Actions			
Issue ID	Issue	Corrective Action	Status of Corrective Action

Software Configuration Management (SCM)

Metrics

Change Request Volume			
Total to Date	Number Reporting Month	% Closed	% Open
24	3	83%	17%

SCM Cost Performance

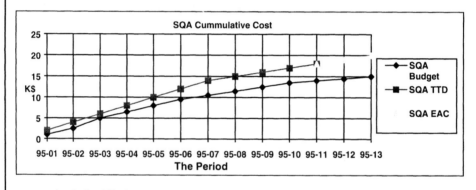

Analysis of Variance

Issues and Corrective Actions

Issues and Corrective Actions			
Issue ID	Issue	Corrective Action	Status of Corrective Action

Customer Satisfaction/Follow-On Potential

In this section of the planning, detail the overall satisfaction of the customer by specific points and areas—note and document any comments and events that demonstrate this satisfaction. One good starting point for reporting on customer satisfaction is to track customer response against the acceptance criteria, as defined at the outset of the project. This will be defined in the Project Charter.

Follow-on potential will see you documenting any new potential business or pending contracts that might become available, together with time frames, amounts, and contacts.

▶ Conclusions

The number of projects that do not have project plans is amazing. IT staff have traditionally complained about the need to produce and manage project plans. Instead of planning their work, these staff members would rather jump right in and immediately start working on a solution or even start writing code. Even worse are those people who believe that a plan is not needed to be successful. These people will never make good project managers.

Project planning must be taken seriously. A project without a plan is similar to a ship without a compass—it might reach its port of destination eventually but numerous deviations from its course and perhaps the risk of foundering on the shoals or rocks must be expected. Even the destination must at least be defined before beginning the journey! Commercial passenger aircraft do not leave any airport in the world without first filing a flight plan. IT projects should be made to conform to the same rigor. *Do not start a project until you have a project plan.*

Project plans have tremendous value. They provide the mechanism for achieving the objectives and deliverables of the project. All plans should be well thought out, structured, and easy to understand.

All plans encounter varying degrees of difficulty, deviations, and unexpected changes. This is a normal process. The key issue here is how many changes? If it is a large number, this might indicate that the plan was not thorough to begin with. Keeping plans accurate requires that project managers keep them up to date.

The time-consuming process of creating a plan that involves resource assignment, budget controls, task assignment, and control intimidates some project managers. They should understand that this is time well spent and will prove valuable when managing throughout the project. Although this chapter was not intended to be a guide on how to develop a comprehensive project plan (truly, there are entire books on the subject!), it is hoped that it has provided a view into the components that are important for successful project planning.

There are three key issues to remember:

1. Plans help to manage the project and guide it to conclusion
2. Plans define a path to be successful
3. Plans prove to be a continuous reference point

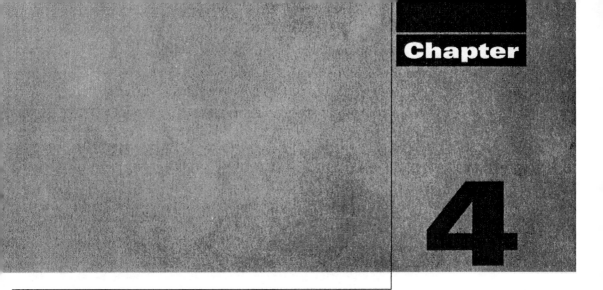

Project Teams

A very essential part of project and resource management is attracting, recruiting, and retaining the best-qualified and capable IT people. Without skilled people, project managers cannot be successful. Since the mid-1970s, there has been a global and continuing shortage of IT staff at all levels. In the late 1990s, it reached serious proportions that required fundamental rethinking and completely different strategic approaches to solving this problem. The demand is increasing through-out the world—in the United States, Europe, Asia, and Central and South America.

▶ Shortages in Information Technology Staff

The shortage in qualified staff is not simply an IT problem; it now affects the entire enterprise, which has become increasingly dependent on technology to sustain and grow profits, and develop and implement new services or products. Chief Executive Officers are now aware of the need to sustain their IT departments in order to maintain the health of their business. Without staffing for IT systems, the corporation may experience major loss of market share, loss of the ability to compete in the fast-moving global economy, loss of opportunity, and the inability to implement new systems fast enough—all of which leads to lower profits. Moreover, this shortage shows no signs of abating in the next

43

10 years and will grow to unmanageable levels in certain regions and countries.

▶ Need for Retention

Historically, the majority of IT organizations have had major difficulties in recruiting and retaining qualified and experienced IT staff. This has been a worldwide phenomenon affecting all major established developed countries with the exception of India, which has a consistent flow of college graduates with which to develop an offshore IT business. Since the computer industry began, IT staff have looked for career development, technical challenges, compensation, and promotion.

The demand for IT staff at all levels of seniority and qualifications has reached unprecedented levels. In simple terms, the demand far outstrips supply. Every level, from programmer to president, is in constant demand. Consider the following statistics:

1. IT staff turnover rates, which, until a few years ago, ran between 5% and 10%, now are running between 10% and 20%—double the figure of not-so-long ago. In the worst-case organizations, it can be as much as 40%.

2. Corporations that attempt to fill internal positions often have long wait times, simply because the skills being sought are not available internally.

3. When employee prospects are found, companies frequently find that they are losing talented resources to the highest bidder, based on total compensation packages that include hefty salaries, signing and performance bonuses, stock option plans, and other "perks." Company loyalty is at an all-time low, and a mercenary attitude among employees is pervasive.

In the chaotic and often frantic world of recruitment, IT staff members have only to pick up the latest copy of any trade magazine to determine their current worth. It has been the experience of this author that IT staff members are keenly aware of what they are worth and have no hesitation in offering their services to the highest bidder. There is a joke that circulated in Silicon Valley for many years that if software engineers do not like their current assignments, they simply leave their driveways in a different direction to find the next job. This author managed on a large project in the mid-1980s with a large contingent of programmers. Career programmers were referred to as "someone who returned after lunch,"—and that was over ten years ago. All of the members of the IT staff, including senior members and, especially, project managers, are possible targets of attractive outside offers. Recruiters compile "hit-lists" of potential candidates, then go after them aggressively to fill positions.

This trend is now worldwide and has reached epidemic proportions in the United States. It is also reaching into areas known for their traditional stable labor markets, such as the Midwestern United States and the United Kingdom.

The loss of project staff means that IT management cannot commit to and deliver on the demands of customers or clients, resulting in unacceptable levels of project delay. Further, the unexpected loss of project staff, often at critical times, can throw project plans, estimates, and milestone deliverables in complete disarray if not planned for.

The list below illustrates some of the reasons why IT staff are in such demand:

- Globalization and the ever expanding corporate need to do business anywhere, anytime, anyhow
- Mergers and Acquisitions—bigger is always better and more profitable
- Joint ventures, partnerships, birth of the Virtual Corporation
- Dramatic increase in magnitude of IT activities worldwide
- Year 2000 (Y2K) crisis created a short-term demand in the mid- 1990s
- The rise and acceptance of the Internet as a place to conduct business
- Rising complexity of IT management issues such as architectures, tools, methodologies
- Unparalleled corporate dependence on IT—can't do business without systems
- Unfulfilled internal corporate training programs
- Continuous and fast changing or emerging technologies

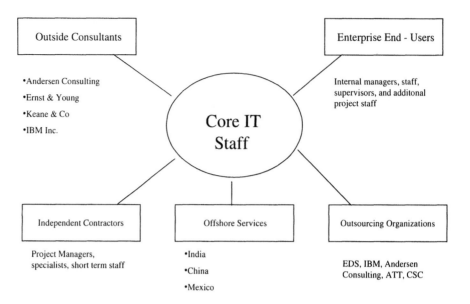

Figure 4–1   The Technology Project Staffing Model.

- Heavy use of corporate application packages—more "buy" than "develop"
- Dramatic increase in outsourcing, partnering and virtual organizations
- Rapid increase in the trend towards independent contractors and consultants
- Application backlog still a significant problem
- Failure of colleges and schools to provide adequate courses

Replacement staff members—if you can locate or find them to begin with—cannot be recruited quickly enough or brought up to speed in time. They often take months to appear. It is not uncommon to hear that some organizations lose as much as 40% of staff annually. The current situation is very serious and is likely to continue this way for the many years.

In response, corporations have had to develop a model that has evolved over time, enabling them to staff projects and make progress, using resources external to the company, as needed. Figure 4–1 illustrates that model. IT management must maintain a core set of managers who possess a strategic set of skills in managing. When a particular set of skills is required, the standard is now to look outside the organization to buy it.

The Cost of Information Technology Staff Replacement—An Analysis

When someone leaves a company to go elsewhere, the cost of replacing that person approaches a prohibitively expensive level. It is expensive not only in terms of monetary costs, but also in the cost of knowledge and experience that the person has and has contributed to the project/corporation.

For key people or content experts, the cost can be even higher. The cost of turnover for the departing person can be as much as 150% to 250% of that person's salary and more for expert knowledge workers.

Consider both the hard and soft cost factors that make up this figure:

1. All of the cost of recruiting to replace the person who is departing, including sign-on bonuses, relocation expenses, temporary travel expenses, training costs, recruitment fees, and advertising expenses.

2. The cost of a temporary contractor, consultant, or other personnel to fill the work gap.

3. All of the costs indicated in 1, above, for the new employee.

4. Learning curve costs for the new employee—typically, a graduated cost of 3–6 months before the new employee becomes fully productive.

5. Salary differences between departing and new employees can be as much as 15% to 40%.

6. The cost of low morale and lost productivity of project teams that have to pick up the slack of departing project team members.

7. Relocation expenses for the new employee and family.

8. Management costs associated with new interviews, training, and administration.

9. New employee training costs and orientation.

The factors listed above may be only a starting point for most corporations, and many will have more specific and individual costs. Many or all of these costs are avoidable if corporations are realistic about keeping people. Many corporations make significant judgments in error by sacrificing employees due to stubbornness over salaries or bonuses. It is a very costly mistake to make in this current climate of recruitment and retention.

IT human resources departments need to be very aware and perform regular assessments on the mood, needs, and direction of how employees feel. They can do this through regular surveys, assessments, web sites, and intranets, and to invite feedback on how to improve the retention of all IT employees. Human resources departments could set up employee councils to exchange information and gauge reactions to new programs or improvements in existing programs.

The basic package of benefits, including health and dental insurance, vision programs, 401K, pension plans, and stock purchase plans, is the absolute minimum needed. However, providing more than the basic package is becoming the norm among companies looking to attract top talent. IT professionals look to other, more flexible benefits, such as flextime and telecommuting, to balance family life with work. Many IT project members would willingly exchange some money for working from home. This particularly applies to project staff with young children. IT project managers and senior staff need to be in touch with their staff members and their needs. Money has always been a motivator. However, this invariably works only in the short term and may not be a total answer to recruitment and retention. Further, to pay IT staff members more money to burn themselves out is not the solution. *The cost of replacing IT people is unacceptably high, compared with the cost of keeping them. Management's attitudes to this problem must change.*

▶ Retention—Meeting Needs

The cost of lost productivity, retraining, and a host of other factors should be sufficient for any IT or project manager to review seriously any new technique to wage war against this crisis. A project manager faced with a resignation needs to get to the real causes, rather than those given by the employee. Often, the real root causes for resignations come from unexpected sources.

Abraham Maslow (1908–1970) was a United States psychologist and behavioral scientist. He spent part of his career in industry, as well as working as an academic. His "Hierarchy of Needs" theory was first presented in 1943 in the publication *U.S. Psychological Review* and later developed in his book, *Motivation and Personality*, first published in 1954. His concepts were originally offered as general explanations of human behavior but quickly became a significant contribution to workplace motivation theory. These concepts are still used by managers today to understand, predict, and influence employee motivation. Maslow was one of the first people to be associated with the humanistic, as opposed to a task-based, approach to management. As people have increasingly come to be appreciated as a key resource in successful companies, Maslow's model has remained a valuable management concept used by many organizations.

Maslow's Hierarchy of Needs Model states that there is a set of psychologic human needs. It defines that all human beings have fundamental necessities and basic requirements, based on a hierarchical process. From very fundamental needs, such as shelter, food, and warmth, it rises in the hierarchy to greater and more substantial needs at different levels. Maslow's diagram, known as *Maslow's Pyramid*, is shown in Figure 4–2. The model asserts that the urge to fulfill a basic need will begin only when a lower need is satisfied. We all have a need for food, shelter, warmth, and we grow to higher needs, once these have been achieved.

Conversely, the reverse will mean that human needs will decline when no longer met, and expectations will be lowered.

Maslow's model also applies to the IT world. For example, IT staff members need to feel secure, and this is often difficult to obtain, given the nature, style, and dynamics of our industry. We often feel a great deal of *insecurity*, due to the rapid pace of change that we cannot control and many other factors, some of which are listed below:

- Employment instability
- Lack of sufficient training
- Need to be part of a team
- Skepticism over a project's success

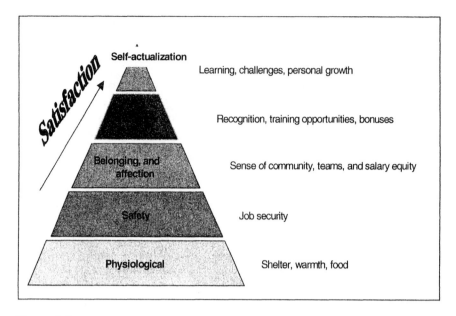

Figure 4–2   Maslow's Pyramid.

- Management frustration
- Financial uncertainty
- New skills uncertainty

At the very highest point, Maslow's model is again strongly associated with the IT industry, where there is a need to attain growth and self-esteem.

To combat the high rate of employee turnover and the expense of replacing key employees, the management of many forward thinking and progressive IT departments is turning to retention packages. These packages are designed to keep existing staff and to create benefits and an environment that is attractive in many forms. The retention package must be flexible, wide ranging, and, most of all, meet the needs of the project team. Project team members must feel that they are valued for their hard work and not feel the urge to jump ship when the next opportunity arises.

The list below is an example of the varying types of benefits that some companies currently offer to retain IT staff:

- Loans for train travel, car parking, and discount travel allowances
- Lower interest mortgages, loans, and saving incentives; student loans for children of employees
- Credit cards with low-interest repayments
- Flexible hours (flextime) schedules; working from home (telecommuting)
- Extra pension, life insurance for employees and all immediate family members
- Paid maternity/paternity leave; extra time off for first-time parents; adoption and foster care grants and assistance
- Starting vacation of four weeks—more for long-term sign-up; vacation accumulation each year
- Flexible personal time and holidays, including individual religious holiday observance (Jewish, Islamic, and other holidays)
- Military and jury duty exceptions
- Comfortable office accommodation with privacy features (no "bullpen"-type cubicles)
- On-site child care centers, shops, dry cleaning, ATM, and full banking facilities
- Quality medical services available, on-site visiting physicians and dentists; free medical, allergy and flu shots, mammograms, PAP smears, X-rays, and travel immunization without leaving the office
- Stock options, bonuses, and incentive plans
- Access to library and research facilities
- Additional family services for babies, young children, and the elderly
- Bereavement leave—extra for international family occasions
- Crisis counseling for cancer, divorce, death, AIDS, and other traumatic events; obesity and weight control counseling
- Free legal advice on consumer and domestic issues
- Free on-site fitness center and deals offering discounts with local centers

- Incentive-based wellness and fitness plans: "stay well, get paid"
- Discounted or subsidized software or computer purchases
- Air travel bargains and vacation discount packages
- Discount dining and entertainment or sports events
- Sabbatical pursuits after a designated period of service to the company and when project time scales permit
- Outside college education and continuing education tuition reimbursement
- On-site car repair and maintenance
- Investment and financial planning services
- Continuing community involvement
- National support or matching programs for United Way, Amnesty International, Red Cross, and other charitable causes

Although the above list may seem excessive to many, IT organizations will often learn the hard way in recognizing these new trends. Also note that money alone is not the answer. People want a variety of benefits that fit their individual needs. Imagine for a moment that you are a potential new recruit to a project and you read the above list as part of the recruitment process. What this means is that retention is vital for attracting new project staff. IT organizations must go above and beyond its competitors, who will be offering similar types of benefits.

▶ Conclusions

Project managers rely on good, qualified staff to help ensure a project's success. Good talent has always been hard to find but, in today's market, it is becoming nearly impossible to find the right people to do the work. Even when they are found, they can be difficult to keep. Other companies need the talent just as much, and they will do anything they can to entice employees away. Needless to say, this has a huge impact on the project manager, who may find that 20–40% of the project staff may change over the course of the project. Companies need to address employee attrition and its impacts on the organization in terms of costs, lost productivity, and dipping corporate morale. Keeping key employees may mean the difference between gaining or keeping competitive advantage—or not.

Early results indicate that, with well-structured retention packages as part of their overall corporate culture, *organizations can expect attrition rates of less than 2%.* This is very significant and verifies the successful approach. It is money well spent.

This author predicts that IT organizations that do not implement retention packages will experience more than triple the amount of project staff turnover than will those that do. Good IT people are hard to find—do everything you can to keep them.

Part 3

The Project Management Lifecycle

5

Project Lifecycle Overview

▶ Introduction

Any information technology organization must have a highly structured framework into which it can place processes, principles, and guidelines. The framework used for software development is a called a *lifecycle*. The software development lifecycle (SDLC) defines a repeatable process for building information systems that incorporate guidelines, methodologies, and standards.

A lifecycle delivers value to an organization by addressing specific business needs within the software application development environment. The implementation of a lifecycle aids project managers in minimizing system development risks, eliminating redundancy, and increasing efficiencies. It also encourages reuse, redesign, and, more importantly, reducing costs.

Purpose

The purpose of the lifecycle is to define the activities involved in the corporation's software application development process and the relationship to various methodologies. This section of the book is

57

targeted toward current and potential project managers for use in software application development projects. The lifecycle and processes defined herein form a corporation's standard practice for software development.

Background

The SDLC is considered a culmination of the effort of project managers who define for themselves the "best practices." This team effort has results in a corporation's ability to leverage its strengths in a continuing effort to deliver world-class software.

This SDLC is a process. The software development organizations of the corporation are the process owners.

Goals

The principle goal of the SDLC is to reduce the corporation's IT costs, cycle time, and time to market while improving the quality of the information systems delivered. The lifecycle details the activities and practices that the project teams follow to plan, build, and deploy new and existing information systems and their applications. Other goals of the SDLC are to:

- Reduce costs of projects by minimizing rework and maintenance efforts
- Reduce cycle time of projects by providing a consistent, repeatable process to follow
- Increase quality of software applications by providing superior solutions that meet customer needs
- Assist project managers in managing projects more effectively
- Provide a framework to help manage project team members, development partners, or subcontractors

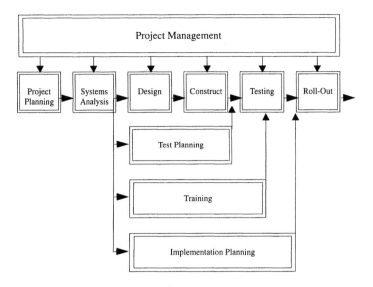

AN EXAMPLE OF A TYPICAL SOFTWARE DEVELOPMENT LIFECYCLE

Figure 5–1   The Software Development Lifecycle.

Overview

Figure 5–1 illustrates the SDLC. This lifecycle provides a defined repeatable process for software development.

The illustration above is a process mapping that depicts phases and exit points (also known as *milestones*) for each phase. As shown, these phases occur in a sequential and/or concurrent fashion. The six development phases are:

1. Project Planning
2. Analysis
3. Design
4. Construction
5. Test
6. Rollout

Three additional phases are performed as concurrent activities. These phases are:

1. Test Planning and Preparation
2. Training Development
3. Implementation Planning

The Test Planning and Preparation Phase begins at the start of the Design Phase and completes before entering the Test Phase. The Training Development Phase begins at the start of the Design Phase and becomes an input to the Test Phase. The Implementation Planning and Preparation Phase begins at the start of the Design Phase and completes before entering the Rollout Phase.

Figure 5–2 depicts the phase activities and their relationship within the SDLC process. This process map also depicts the deliverables from each phase.

Each of these phases is discussed in further detail in subsequent chapters.

In addition to an SDLC, an IT organization needs to control project management, release/change management, and production environments. These are additional processes that are highly interdependent on the SDLC. These management-related processes are not covered by this book, and there is a need to develop and construct separate templates to manage these important activities.

▶ Lifecycle Process Management

Stakeholders

The term *stakeholders* refers to participants in the project that have an interest in its outcome. The following are considered stakeholders in the planning, management, and implementation of the SDLC process:

- Project managers and their teams

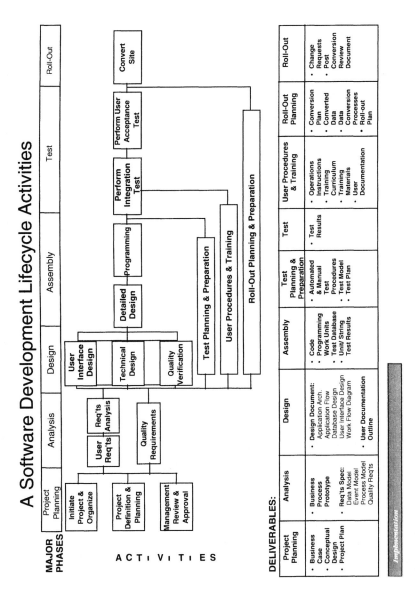

A Software Development Lifecycle Activities

MAJOR PHASES	Project Planning	Analysis	Design	Assembly	Test	Roll-Out

Project Planning: Initiate Project & Organize · Project Definition & Planning · Management Review & Approval

Analysis: User Req'ts Analysis · Quality Requirements

Design: User Interface Design · Technical Design · Quality Verification

Assembly: Detailed Design · Programming

Test: Perform Integration Test · Perform User Acceptance Test

Roll-Out: Convert Site

Test Planning & Preparation

User Procedures & Training

Roll-Out Planning & Preparation

ACTIVITIES

DELIVERABLES:

Project Planning	Analysis	Design	Assembly	Test Planning & Preparation	Test	User Procedures & Training	Roll-Out Planning	Roll-Out

• Business Case
• Conceptual Design
• Project Plan
	• Business Process Prototype
	• Req'ts Spec:
	  Data Model
	  Event Model
	  Process Model
	  Quality Reqts
		• Design Document:
		  Application Arch.
		  Application Flow
		  Database Design
		  User Interface Design
		  Work Flow Diagram
		• User Documentation Outline
			• Code
			• Programming Work Units
			• Test Database
			• Unit/ String Test Results
				• Automated & Manual Test Procedures
				• Test Model
				• Test Plan
					• Test Results	• Operations Instructions
						• Training Curriculum
						• Training Materials
						• User Documentation
							• Conversion Plan
							• Converted Data
							• Data Conversion Processes
							• Roll-out Plan
								• Change Requests
								• Post Conversion Review Document

Figure 5–2 Software Development Lifecycle Activities and Deliverables.

- Application Development Management (ADM)
- Information Technology Senior Management (CIOs)
- Information Technology Architecture (ITA) Software Lifecycle Implementation Organization or similar organization
- Clients, interested end users

Audience

The audience for SDLC includes:

- Project managers
- Stakeholders described above
- All of the corporation's IT application development organizations
- The corporation's IT support and operations organizations (help desks, network support services)
- The corporation's training organization
- The corporation's external partners (consulting, contractors, vendors)
- IT Senior and Executive Management

Roles and Responsibilities

A Software Lifecycle Implementation group is needed to champion and manage the implementation of the Software Development Lifecycle throughout the corporation. They are tasked with communicating the lifecycle, consulting with project managers in support of the lifecycle, monitoring its effectiveness and maintaining the structure and content of the lifecycle. This effort also includes incorporating lessons learned and new concepts into the lifecycle and designing future releases.

Revision Process

Any individual from any of the corporation's IT organizations may request modifications or offer suggestions to the SDLC. It is only by continuous evolution that this process will become effective and add value to the corporation. The stakeholders will meet, as appropriate, to review the revisions requested and either approve, deny, or charter a study for each request. Approved revisions will be reflected in the next release. Teams consisting of project managers and team members from application development organizations throughout the corporation will continually be asked to participate in reviews.

New Releases

Release management will be used as required, and a schedule will be approved and released. Issuance of new releases will be coordinated through the stakeholders.

Communication

The Standard Development Lifecycle (SDL) will be communicated throughout the organization, the business area teams, the corporation's internal web home page, and through distribution of printed copies to stakeholders. Notification of new releases will be done via e-mail and paper mail to the stakeholders, various internal corporate publications, newsletters, and other appropriate methods of communications.

▶ Section Layout and Structure

This section of the book is broken into phases that further define each of the components of the SDLC. The following details are provided for each phase:

- Process mapping—A detailed process flow of activities
- Purpose—A brief overview of the phase
- Objectives—The key components necessary to complete the phase
- Activities—The actions required to complete the phase
- Roles—The necessary skill sets for the phase

- Inputs—The components required to begin the phase
- Outputs (deliverables)—The components as a result of a phased activity
- Milestones—Specific events that occur during and/or upon completion of a phase

▶ Phase Checklists

Phase manager checklists contain phase exit criteria that can be used by a project to ensure completion of phase activity. These checklists provide the means to facilitate phase walk-through and reviews. Each checklist defines the exit criteria for a particular phase. The checklists should be used by project managers and their teams to monitor the progress of a project, both within a phase and through the various phases, to ensure that quality issues are addressed and resolved, rather than overlooked or deferred. These checklists should serve as a baseline and may be expanded for specific project issues and deliverables.

Individual work products (deliverables) may pass from one phase to another at different times. A phase is not considered complete until *all* work products have passed and all negotiated open issues are closed.

Table 5–1 describes the items contained in the checklists.

Table 5–1   Phase Checklists

Item	Descriptions
Change Request (CR) Number	Information on the CR(s) that this package is related to
Release number	Name of the release this package is related to
Deliverables	Deliverables needed to exit a phase and begin a new one
	• For each methodology-defined deliverable, indicate whether it is present (Yes) or not (No), or whether it is not applicable (N/A) under these circumstances. If No or N/A, Comments must be filled in to show why the phase can be considered complete without the deliverable.
	• Each Project should add any Project-specific deliverables to the checklist.

(continued)

Table 5–1 Phase Checklists *(continued)*

Item	Descriptions
Quality Checkpoints	Checkpoints needed to ensure that all deliverables are complete and accurate.
	• For Quality milestone, indicate whether it is present (Yes) or not (No), or whether it is not applicable (N/A) under these circumstances. If No or N/A, Comments must be filled in to show why the phase can be considered complete without the milestone.
	• Entrance Criteria review should *always* be done for each phase. Although Exit Criteria for preceding phases may have been signed off, the team should review the status activities at the beginning of a phase as a quality issue. This is especially important in the Rollout Phase, where inputs from three different phases are required for entrance.
	• Each Project should add any Project-specific milestones to the list.
Working Checklist	Indicates different deliverables for the project and the person who is primarily responsible for the production of the deliverable. Due Date and Initials indicate that the deliverable is complete and available for review and use. Doc Ref indicates the name/location of supporting documentation for the deliverable. A project should add open issues and items to check, as needed, to ensure that complete coverage of the area is provided.
Open Issues	An area where open issues covered during exit negotiations can be documented. When requirements have not been fully met but there is general agreement that the project should move forward, they should be listed here. This should include a proposed resolution date and responsible party. All parties must agree to this before having a valid exit from the phase.
Sign-off	Area where all responsible parties indicate their agreement that the phase has been successfully completed and that the project should move into the next phase.
Sending Team	Team leader or Manager responsible for the phase being exited sign, indicating their agreement that everything is complete.
Sending Architect	The Project or Phase Architect signs, indicating agreement that everything is complete.

(continued)

Table 5–1   Phase Checklists *(continued)*

Item	Descriptions
Receiving Team	Sign-off indicates that affected recipients have a completed package and that all open issues have been discussed, assigned, and recorded with target resolution dates. This may include other Project phases, the Customer/Sponsor, or other systems that will need to interface with the new system. Recipients have the right to decline sign-off when appropriate.

▶ CRUD—Deliverables Matrix

A CRUD (Create, Read, Update, Delete) matrix is a cross-reference of the deliverables created during the SDLC process. The matrix in Figure 5–3 identifies the relationship between a deliverable and the phases responsible for its creation, review, and/or update. The description for each deliverable can be found within the corresponding phase in which it was created. This matrix can be used to follow the progression of a deliverable through the phases of the SDLC process.

DELIVERABLES	PROJECT PLANNING	ANALYSIS	DESIGN	ASSEMBLY	USER PROC. & TRAINING	TEST PLAN & PREP	TEST	ROLL-OUT PLAN	ROLL-OUT
Automated & Manual Test Procedures						C			
Business Case	C	RU	R	R	R	R	R	R	R
Business Process Prototype		C	R						C
Change Requests							R		
Code				C					
Conceptual Design	C	R							
Conversion Plan						R		C	R
Converted Data								C	R
Data Conversion Processes					R	R		C	
Design Document			C	R	R	R		R	
Application Architecture			C					R	
Application Flow			C						
Database Design			C	R		R		R	
User Interface Design			C	R	R				
Work Flow Diagram			C	R	R	R			
Operations Instructions					C				R
Post Conversion Review Doc.									C
Project Plan	C	RU	RU	RU	RU	RU	RU	RU	RU
Requirements Specification		C	R			R			
Data Model		C	R			R			
Event Model		C	R			R			
Process Model		C	R			R			
Quality Requirements		C	R			R			
Roll-Out Plan								C	R
Test Database				C					
Test Model						C	R		
Test Plan						C	R		
Test Results							CR		
Training Curriculum					CR				
Training Materials					CR				
Unit/String Test Results				CR					
User Documentation					C		R		R
User Documentation Outline			C		R				

Legend:
C = Created in Phase
R = Reviewed in Phase
U = Updated/Modified in Phase

Figure 5-3 CRUD Matrix

Project Planning Phase

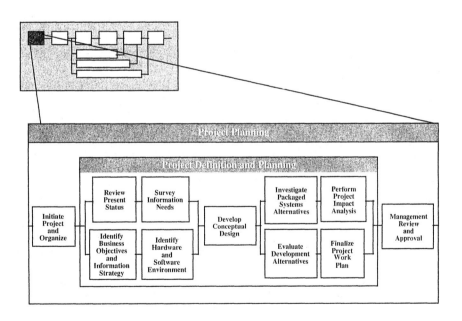

▶ Purpose

The purpose of the Project Planning Phase is to identify information technology requirements stemming from business objectives. An action plan or work breakdown structure (WBS) is then developed to define specific projects to achieve the identified information technology goals. In this phase, the development approach, benefits, and a reasonable estimate of the development costs of the conceptual design are determined. The process map above depicts the activities required to complete the Project Planning Phase.

▶ Objectives

The key activities for the planning phase are as follows:

- Project Initiation—Plan for the start of the project
- Identify user needs, system performance requirements and features, current technology infrastructure, existing information strategy, future technology considerations, and the impact or gap analysis on related systems
- Develop the conceptual design of the new system
- Evaluate factors, such as (but not limited to) scope, cost, schedule, resources, staffing, and training
- Analyze risk and benefits, and consider alternative solutions
- Develop and approve the project plan
- Document the business case to present to management that justifies the new system

Each of these steps is explained in further detail in the following section.

▶ Activities

Initiate Project and Organize

This task includes the work required to obtain management approval for the project and subsequent planning of the work effort. This involves identifying the scope of the project, the applicable standards for the project, the outputs of the project, development of the project plan, and organization and training of the project team.

Project Definition and Planning

This activity includes the development of the project definition and the planning and estimation involved in the system's conceptual design.

Review Present Status

The existing information system can provide valuable input to the project team. Reviewing the current system helps the project team to understand the environment in which the new system will operate. If an existing system will be replaced, its strengths, weaknesses, functions, and features are useful in developing specifications for the new system. The overall quality of existing systems and past experience in their development indicates capabilities for developing the new system.

Identify Business Objectives and Information Strategy

All systems development projects should help to achieve overall business and information objectives. A review of business and information plans identifies these requirements and guidelines affecting the new system. Strategies within the plan also show the hardware and software environment in which the new system will operate.

One frequent challenge encountered when beginning a new project is that the project is defined by the technology that an organization wishes to implement, rather than the business problem or issue it is trying to solve. For example, a company manager may say "we want to develop a web site" without identifying *why* it may be necessary to do that. Does this company want to provide marketing materials to its geographically distributed sales force or sell products or services via the web? One implementation of this "requirement" might dictate the development of a static HTML-based "brochureware" site, and the other requires an e-commerce solution. The technologies, tools, and team skills are widely different for each of these projects. The impact to the organization as a result of these disparate projects is different, too. One project might see no change or an increase in the number of people in the sales force as information can be better rolled out. The other might see a decrease in the number of salespeople as more sales are brought in through the web. So you see, defining the business objective is key to understanding what you are trying to build and has an impact on how you are going to build it.

Survey Information Needs

The information needs and requirements of end users are determined by the functions that they perform in their business units and the decisions that they make. After assessing functional, technical, and information processing trends, the project team develops a going-in position on the new system. This going-in position is based on expectations of information needs, major inputs and outputs, and on the required performance and security levels.

Identify Hardware and Software Environment

To develop the conceptual design of the new system, the project team needs to know its expected hardware and software environments. The environment will also affect the development approach to be used. Using work documents relating to present status and information strategies, the project team describes the expected environment in these areas. Where choices exist, an environment is selected for the new system.

Develop Conceptual Design

Once information needs are identified and the hardware and software environments are reviewed, the conceptual design can be produced. This design includes the business functions to be supported by the new system, the data to be maintained, the system architecture, and the interfaces with other systems. This is based on the information needs of end users and the expected hardware and software environments. Human factors issues and approaches must be addressed in the conceptual design. The goal is to be able to communicate the basic functionality and behaviors of the new system and to use this design as a discussion tool for reaching agreement on the project's parameters.

Investigate Packaged Systems Alternatives

This activity confirms the use of purchased software, a custom development approach or a combination of the two. Using the conceptual design as a reference, the project team screens software and identifies those packages most likely to meet the system's requirements. The result is a short list of commercially available packages that will be evaluated during the analysis phase. A final selection of packaged systems is deferred until that phase, when more detailed requirements are available.

Evaluate Development Alternatives

The project team determines how the design and implementation of the system will take place. Decisions are made on the general project team composition, use of development aids, use of prototypes, etc. The development approach is another key input needed to prepare the project work plan.

Prepare Project Impact Analysis

The project team prepares a summary of the costs and benefits of the proposed system. With user assistance, they determine risks and organizational impacts associated with the project. Management must have this information before it can decide whether to proceed with the project.

Finalize Project Work Plan

The team develops the work plans for the analysis and design phases and cost estimates. Information needed to develop the work plan and cost estimates has been gathered throughout the project to this point. The information gathered includes major processing functions, major inputs and outputs, general definition of the databases, a high-level system schematic, various estimates, and assumptions appropriate for the environment. Upon completion of this activity, all information necessary to move into the next phase of systems development is available.

Management Review and Approval

The project team reviews and presents the project definition and planning outputs to management. Included in the presentation is the conceptual design of the proposed system and the scope, timing, cost, and work plan of the subsequent analysis and design phases. If management approves the work performed based on the presentation and the conceptual design, the project team receives authorization to continue with the analysis and design phase.

▶ Roles

Team members involved at this stage are:

> **Customer:** usually the ultimate user of the system under development
>
> **Business Process Analyst:** the project team member responsible for understanding the business functions the system is intended to support and for communicating how the new system will behave
>
> **Executive Sponsor:** the member of the organization's executive management who champions the project. This is a role that is critical to the ultimate success of the project.
>
> **Project Management:** the individual or group of individuals responsible for the day-to-day management of the project

▶ Inputs

Information Plan

This plan provides the high-level description of the enterprise's information systems and related business objectives. This plan is most often a narrative document, sometimes with charts, graphs, or diagrams.

▶ Outputs

Business Case

The business case provides the justification for the system and project decisions developed during the project planning phase. The business case becomes the established framework within which to evaluate system and project-related issues, changes, and enhancements. The business case becomes the baseline set of business objectives used to manage and guide the project.

Conceptual Design

A high-level design of a system is prepared before any development starts. The conceptual design does not commit the team to details. Rather, it serves as input to the development plan and the business case. The conceptual design is intended to function as a "paper model" of the system to be developed and should be used to talk through and reach agreement on what is proposed prior to actually building the system. The form of the conceptual design can vary, depending on the preferred mode of communication, the system to be developed, and the sophistication of the audience. For example, the conceptual design might consist of a narrative document, a storyboard of how the system is supposed to look, function and feel, or a series of diagrams; most likely, however, it may be a combination of all of these elements.

Project Plan

Project managers will need a plan that defines and details the project organizational structure, approach, scope, project-specific standards, resource and staffing plans, work elements, work plan, program milestones, configuration management strategy, and software quality assurance objectives and goals. The project plan also includes the development environment description, risk and issues management strategy, metric goals and collection and reporting techniques, and tools used during the project.

▶ Milestones

Project Plan Sign-Off

The Project Plan sign-off indicates management's approval for the project to proceed as specified in the project plan. In addition, because the project plan is used throughout the SDLC, it may be necessary to perform periodic updates (and re-reviews and approvals) to maintain an accurate reflection of project activity.

▶ Tools

There are numerous tools used in this phase to create the necessary deliverables, as well as any intermediate work documents. Some of these deliverables will require, or at least justify, specialized tools, whereas others will make use of standard tools, such as word processing software, presentation tools, and spreadsheets.

Project Planning Software: Used to develop project schedules and resource plans, and Gantt and Pert charts. The most popular project planning tool is Microsoft Project, but other tools, such as Primavera, QSS, or Project Workbench, are also frequently used. Although not a project planning tool, Microsoft Excel is often used to show project schedules.

Project Estimating Software: The project plan and resource list becomes the input for the project estimate. Many project planning tools can help with this step, but frequently a spreadsheet tool, such as Microsoft Excel or Lotus 1-2-3, is used for developing project estimates. Spreadsheets are also used extensively, along with word processors, in the development of cost-benefit analysis and project impact documents.

Analysis and Design Phases

▶ Analysis Phase

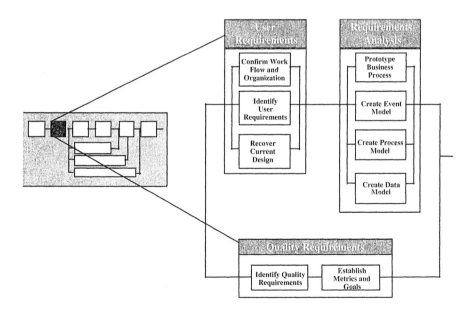

▶ Purpose

The purpose of the Analysis Phase is to formulate and formalize the system's requirements. This is accomplished by establishing what the system is to do, according to the requirements and expectations of the system's end users. The modeling of these requirements is then performed in the form of business, data, event, and process models to demonstrate the understanding of the requirements. This enables the developers and customers to move forward under the same set of expectations with respect to scope and requirements. The process map above depicts the high-level activities required to complete the Analysis Phase.

▶ Objectives

The key objectives for this phase are as follows:

- Build user ownership of the system
- Transform current business models into models of the future system
- Ensure that the scope remains aligned with the business case and is managed appropriately
- Obtain user and sponsor consensus on the system's functionality so that the scope will be stable during the Design and Construction Phases

▶ Activities

End User Requirements

The project team must understand and document the changed organization and the new overall workflow in which the new system will operate. To do this, the current system is analyzed to the degree necessary to understand the changes required and to document those elements that will not change. The project team identifies and describes user requirements in terms of the new system and the differences between the old and new systems. The requirements come from end users during facilitated Joint Application Development (JAD) sessions and one-on-one interviews, factual analysis, and many other techniques, as appropriate. If very fast requirements are necessary, Rapid Application Development (RAD) may be used. See Chapter 13 for more specific details.

Confirm Work Flow and Organization Prepare or confirm documentation about the organization, for example, business processes, structure, and information plans. This documentation, which addresses both current operations and plans for the future, helps the project team to understand the context of the new system.

Identify User Requirements Interview end users to understand what the new system must do to satisfy their needs. Plan and conduct interviews (including JAD sessions, where appropriate), review existing system documentation, and perform a gap analysis to determine the differences between the current and new systems, and the changes required. The requirements must be defined sufficiently to ensure testability. Review the requirements, once drafted, with the end users to ensure that the information has been accurately captured and properly documented.

Recover Current Design The database, file designs, programs, and interfaces of the current system are reviewed. This information will be used to define interfaces between new and existing components of the system.

Quality Requirements

Describe how well the system will carry out its functions. Analyze and break down the four generic quality requirements (performance, reliability, usability, and flexibility) into more detailed and quantitative requirements. Next, a method of measurement and a goal are set for each quality requirement. The quality requirements are ranked, creating tradeoff guidelines when the quality goals are incompatible among themselves or with the budget and the implementation schedule.

Identify Quality Requirements Review the user requirements and the project's cost and schedule. Using these requirements, identify design attributes in four categories: performance, reliability, usability and flexibility. The requirements identified must also be testable. The project sponsor provides criteria for prioritizing these quality requirements.

Establish Metrics and Goals The project team must be able to determine whether the quality requirements have been met. Therefore, establish measures by decomposing the quality attributes into single measurable attributes. Then, based on established goals, determine current achievement levels as a benchmark for comparing future achievement levels.

Requirements Analysis and Management

Analyzing the system requirements is done to deepen understanding of them and to begin translating them into a system design. Requirements analysis allows designers to understand what the system must do to meet user requirements. Three models of the requirements are formalized in parallel: the event model (specifying the system's behavior as viewed from the outside), the data model (specifying the structure of the information maintained by the system), and the process model (describing the system from the inside). These are described in greater detail in the sections that follow.

A prototype or a model of the business process is also often created at this point to ensure that both the end users and the project team thoroughly understand the user requirements already formulated. Because many people have difficulty visualizing abstract concepts or new technology solutions, the prototype also ensures that the user requirements are feasible, testable, and fulfill the end users' needs by providing them something concrete to see and sometimes even interact with.

Prototype Business Process

The purpose of this step is to create and iterate a description of the new business process. The process model is a description of the conceptual data and process flows of the future application. This model is composed of a leveled set of data flow diagrams or a business function decomposition, supported by elementary process descriptions where required.

Often, the prototype can be used as a "living" process model. After defining the scope of the prototype, the next steps are to design and

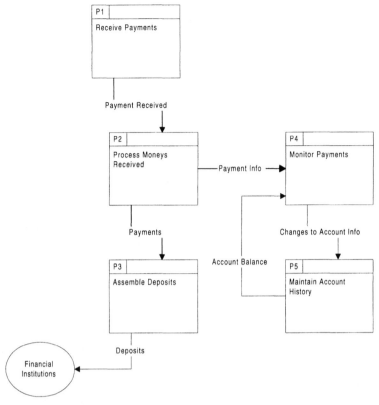

Figure 7–1 A Sample Process Flow Diagram.

build it. Then the project team demonstrates the prototype to selected end users and documents their responses. The project team iterates the prototype as necessary to gain user approval and to help end users take ownership of the new system.

For a limited system, the prototype method is a good way to simulate business behavior. For more complex systems or those larger in scope, however, the prototype method may not be feasible. For these larger systems, the process model is usually communicated using a variety of narrative documents and graphics, such as process flow charts, such as the one shown in Figure 7–1. The purpose of the graphics is to show the flow of the business processes, and the narrative documents provide the detail of each process, including elements such as inputs, outputs, and steps in the process. The process model is continually refined and decomposed until the lowest-level process in the system is fully defined. As with the prototype, the process model diagram is reviewed iteratively with the system end users until agreement is reached that it represents the business processes accurately and completely.

Create Event Model

In this step, the project team creates a model of the business transactions and events involved in the external behavior of the application and verifies the accuracy of the model with selected end users. The event model is a description of the future application according to the external events (business transactions and timer events) that it will process and the responses that the processing will result in. This model is composed of event-stimulus-response descriptions, entity lifecycle diagrams, and, optionally, an entity by events matrix.

Create Data Model

Create a model of the application's data requirements that will be used later to design database and file structures. The data model consists of an entity-relationship diagram and detailed descriptions of each entity, relationship, attribute and data type expected in the new system. From this, the new system's data structures will be built. It is important to verify the accuracy of the model with selected end users. However, many end users are not familiar with data model diagrams, so the project manager may need to provide a significant amount of coaching and orientation before the users are able to participate easily in this review.

A data model excerpt for the previous process model appears in Figure 7–2.

▶ Roles

Project team members involved at this stage include (new ones since the previous chapter are defined here, as well):

Business Process Analyst

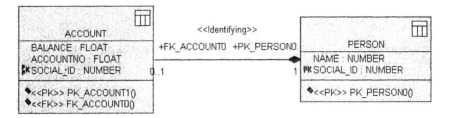

Figure 7–2 A Sample Data Model Excerpt.

Customer

Data Analyst: the data analyst is responsible for understanding and describing the pieces of information that are used in the business and are needed to satisfy the business requirements of the new system.

Human Factors Specialist: an expert in the area of understanding of how people interact with and use computer systems.

Project Management

Subject Matter Expert (SME): a designated expert in his or her particular areas of the business. As an expert, his or her input and feedback is highly valuable and is used to confirm and validate the models, prototype behavior, and, ultimately, the system design.

Tester: responsible for testing the prototype and ensuring that it is functioning correctly as designed.

▶ Inputs

Conceptual Design

A high-level design of a system prepared before development starts. The conceptual design depicts the new system, showing its scope, overall architecture, and relationship to other systems. The conceptual design is a deliverable prepared in the previous Project Planning phase.

Current System Description

The current system description may include database and file designs, program documentation, and/or program code.

Enterprise Model

The enterprise model depicts the conceptual processes, entities, and relationships of interest to the entire enterprise. Neither detailed nor complete, it is a vehicle for communicating with system sponsors and user management about system plans. Each individual development project typically covers only a subset of the enterprise model.

Information Plan

This plan provides the high-level description of the enterprise's informational systems and related business objectives.

▶ Outputs

Business Process Prototype

The business process prototype illustrates how a system will work. The scope of the prototype should concentrate on essential or problematic portions of the system. There are different types of prototypes; the type used will be determined by the goal of the prototyping effort. For example, the goals may be testing conversation flow or system usability.

Requirements Specification

The requirements specification includes and/or provides reference to the data model, event model, process model, and quality requirements.

In addition to the definitions of the data, event, and process models described earlier, the quality requirements are explained here:

Quality Requirements

The quality requirements for the application are expressed as a series of measurable quality attributes, together with the level of achievement to be attained by the application. In addition, they include guidelines for trading off one quality attribute against another (or against cost and implementation schedules).

▶ Milestones

Architecture Analysis Assessment Complete (Optional)

An architecture assessment is a checkpoint conducted between the project team and an independent team to examine, in depth, the project's software, hardware, and underlying technology to provide guidance on enterprise strategies and standard environments. This is a quality assurance mechanism for the software delivery process. This assessment may be considered optional.

Requirements Sign-Off

The customer signs off on the requirement specification: event model, data model, process model, and quality requirements.

▶ Tools

There are numerous tools used in this phase to create the necessary deliverables, as well as any intermediate work documents. Some of these deliverables will require, or at least justify, specialized tools, whereas others will make use of standard tools, such as word processing software, presentation tools, and spreadsheets.

Data Modeling Tools: Used to develop entity-relationship diagrams and/or the detailed descriptions of the components of the data model or data dictionary. Popular tools include those from Rational Software (Rational Rose), Platinum Software, Sterling, and Cayenne. Another popular Microsoft Windows-based tool, Logic Works ER win, is a reasonably inexpensive, simple-to-use program for systems that are not massively complex or large in scope.

Process and Event Modeling Tools: Many of the same vendors that provide data modeling tools also provide modules or complementary products that perform process modeling and systematic decomposition. Visio is also frequently used to create process diagrams, along with a word processor, such as Microsoft Word, to create narrative text about the process details.

▶ Design Phase

Purpose

The purpose of the design portion of the Analysis and Design Phases is to plan out a system that meets those requirements defined in the Analysis stage. The goal of the design stage is to have defined a means of implementing the project solution without actually having implemented it. The process map opening this chapter depicts the high-level activities required to complete the design stage.

Objectives

The key objectives for this stage are as follows:

- Design the user interface: business process flows, dialog and transaction screens, reports, and documents.
- Ensure that the design fulfills the functional requirements, both for the business process and for all the necessary support activities.
- Ensure that the design fulfills the quality requirements, especially usability and reliability (security and controls).

Activities

End User Interface Design

Design the part of the new system as seen by its end users. The driving activity is the design of the user interaction mechanisms, including screens and transaction and information flows, from which individual windows and other inputs and outputs are designed. Finally, the details of the workflow (for example, within the work group or department) are defined.

Design Conversations The high-level design of the human–computer interface begins with a review of the workflow of the business function. This model is used as a basis for developing the human–computer conversations that the system presents to the user in the form of screen sequences and command/response sequences. The conversation design needs to support the business functions, processes, and their related events. At this stage, if not already done, it is important to establish standard conversation types that support a common user interface approach.

Design Screens Create screen layouts that are consistent with the conversation design. Lay out the system's screens completely and define their navigation and interchange, making sure they conform to aesthetic and practical requirements. This design can be done using storyboards and diagrams or the screens can be prototyped, using the same tools with which the actual systems dialogs will be created.

Design Reports and Documents Lay out the reports and documents generated by the application. Standardize where possible, and try to reuse layouts from other applications. As with the screen design, the same tools with which the final reports will be created can often be used for report design. Alternatively, text editors or word processors can be reasonable stand-in tools, if necessary. When using a word processor as a layout tool, it is a good idea to use the same font and point size in the mockup as will be used in the final reports to avoid any later layout problems when the real reports are built.

Technical Design

The project team must define the application architecture. This includes mapping the requirements to the components of the technical architecture and the global design decisions that make up the standards and guidelines for designing the detailed components of the system. If applicable, data and processes are distributed across the network. Programs are identified and decomposed into modules. Interprogram and intermodule messages are designed, as are interfaces to external systems. The data model is transformed first into a logical, then a physical database design.

Define Application Architecture

Define the interrelationship of functional components within the application and how those components will interact with the systems. These decisions have the effect of reducing the complexity of subsequent development decisions, and they help to ensure that quality requirements will be met. Review the architectural model to ensure that it is appropriate in size, quality, and operational ability, and that it is responsive to the business requirements. Resolve any architectural issues by weighing quality requirements against development and maintenance costs and timeframes and, if necessary, gaining agreement and support from the project sponsor or other key management.

Define Processing Flow

Expand on the overall design by identifying the programs to be created, and define in detail the sequence in which processing is

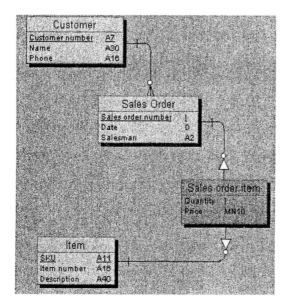

Figure 7-3 A Sample Logical Database Design.

performed and how data is passed between processes. As with other steps in the project so far, creating diagrams or storyboards of program flow is a useful documentation and communication tool.

Design Logical Database/Data Structure

Logical database/data structure design transforms the data model created by Requirements Analysis into logical data structures that are supported by the data management software. This activity designs and documents the database and/or data structures as they will be viewed by application developers and end users.

A logical database or data structure design defines all the individual elements of data that is stored by the new system. Logical data model diagrams show each data item and any dependencies that exist between them. An example of a logical data model appears in Figure 7-3:

Design Automated Processes

Develop sufficient detail to estimate the application's costs, resource consumption, and response times. Design each program by decomposing it into lower-level modules. Describe each module's purpose and processing rules. Design the system's program according to the program packages. Develop database access patterns and other I/O operations.

Design System Interfaces

Design the interface between the application that is being built and other systems with which it will communicate (for example, a shared database, a transaction file interface, or on-line transmission of individual messages). As necessary, create change requests to modify existing systems.

Design Physical Database/Data Structure

Specify the physical storage and access structures that will help to ensure optimal performance and reliability. The physical design of the data structure depends greatly on the specific technology chosen. For example, the physical data structure for an Oracle database differs greatly from that of one using data found in a system file. Usually, the physical design is created using the package-specific scripting language or a text/file editor that can be read by the package.

Quality Verification and Validation (QV&V)

End users and technical personnel verify and validate that the design includes all of the functional requirements and that the quality requirement goals are likely to be met. Special attention should be given to usability and performance.

Verify Functional Completeness

Ensure that the design meets functional (or user) requirements and that each functional requirement has been incorporated into one or more design objects (programs, processes, data, etc.).

Test and Verify Quality Attributes

Ensure that the design meets the quality requirements: performance, reliability, usability, flexibility, project cost, and schedule.

▶ Roles

Project team members involved at this stage include (new ones since the previous chapter are defined here, as well):

Business Process Analyst

Customer

Data Analyst

Designer: responsible for portions of the designed elements or for the design overall. Is knowledgeable about the design of user interfaces, system interaction, data models.

Human Factors Specialist

Project Management

Subject Matter Expert (SME)

Technical Architect

End User

▶ Inputs

Corporate Standards

All corporations need Application Development standards. These standards include, but are not limited to, the *IT Standard Environment* standards. These standards specify products and technologies, as well as release levels and IT architecture that will be used for the enterprise. It also contains architecture strategies, platforms, networks, and protocols for different computing areas. The standards should be used within the SDL to provide guidelines on the application of the technology to the new system. If no standards exist or are not applicable, the project team has additional work in designing and testing the new technologies.

Business Process Prototype

The business process prototype illustrates how a system will work. The prototype also concentrates on essential or problematic portions of the system.

Requirements Specification

The requirements specification includes and/or provides reference to the data model, event model, process model, and quality requirements.

▶ Outputs

Design Document

The design document includes and/or references the application architecture, application flow, database design, user interface design, and the workflow diagram. The descriptions for these are as specified below:

Application Architecture

The application architecture takes the form of a set of overall decisions that are documented by mapping the functional requirements of the application to its technical architecture (program packaging models and architecture primitives) and to a set of design standards.

Application Flow

The application flow portrays the overall flow of information through the system. It graphically displays all programs (on-line, asynchronous, and batch) and all interprogram communications (files and databases) for the application and its outside interfaces.

Database Design

The database design is in two parts: the logical design (the programmers' and end users' views) and the physical database design (the database administrator's view).

End User Interface Design

The user interface design covers user interactions at the workstation (dialogs and screens for block-mode terminals, dialogs and windows for intelligent workstations) and outside the workstation (reports and other objects).

Workflow Diagram

Workflow diagrams are used to document automated process designs and manual workflow designs.

The automated process design is the description of executables and modules of the application. This description depicts how data and control flows from one executable to another.

The manual workflow design covers the nonautomated part of the business process: input preparation, report distribution, workstation operation, error correction and reentry, workflow control, performance, security, and controls.

User Documentation Outline

The user documentation outline records the manual processes to be developed and how they will be organized.

▶ Milestones

Architecture Design Assessment Complete

An architecture assessment is a checkpoint conducted between the project team and an independent team to examine, in depth, the project's software, hardware, and underlying technology to ensure compliance with enterprise strategies and standard environments. This is a quality assurance mechanism for the software delivery process. This assessment may be combined with the lifecycle assessment if both are desired.

Design Sign-Off

The design document is signed off, indicating the approval of the completed system design. The approval is obtained from all affected roles or stakeholders before construction can proceed. This includes the end users' approval of the user interface and detailed workflow.

Lifecycle Assessment Complete

A lifecycle assessment is a formal review of a project's status conducted between the project team and an independent team to identify risk areas and propose actions to address those risks. It focuses on the project from a management viewpoint. This is a quality assurance mechanism for the software delivery process. The lifecycle assessment is recommended for new development projects, as well as for re-engineering efforts with greater than a 50% change.

▶ Tools

There are numerous tools used in this stage to create the necessary deliverables, as well as any intermediate work documents. Some of these deliverables will require, or at least justify, specialized tools, whereas others will make use of standard tools, such as word processing software, presentation tools, and spreadsheets.

Data Modeling Tools: Used to develop the logical data model or data dictionary. Popular and useful tools include those from Rational Software (Rational Rose), Platinum Software, Logic Works ER/win or ER/Studio, Sterling and Cayenne.

Process and Event Modeling Tools: Many of the same vendors that provide data modeling tools also provide modules or complementary products that perform process modeling and systematic decomposition. Visio is also frequently used to create process diagrams, along with a word processor, such as Microsoft Word, to create narrative text about the process details.

Construction Phase

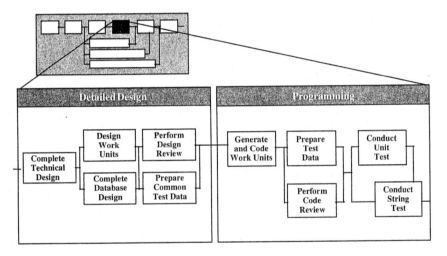

▶ Purpose

The purpose of the Construction Phase is to complete the detailed design of the required architectures (development, execution, and operations) and to build the application or system using the agreed-upon development environment and tools. Developers create the desired application using the design documents as their guide. The process map above depicts the activities required to complete the Construction Phase.

▶ Objectives

The key objectives for this phase are as follows:

- Prepare and complete the detailed design for all portions of the system and the conversion effort
- Create executable modules
- Test individual modules
- Integrate components
- Perform intermodule testing (string testing)

▶ Activities

Detailed Design

Using the technical design as a guide, prepare detailed documentation for each work unit. *Work unit* refers to a logical chunk of the project that can be designed and developed independently from another part of the project, then later integrated as needed. Many projects consist of multiple smaller subprojects that can be run in parallel, which can significantly accelerate the project speed and release schedule but also adds significantly to the complexity of project management.

After completing the detailed documentation for the work unit, document the logical data views and physical data structures in each programming work unit and communicate them to programmers. The analyst should walk through the design with all appropriate project team members. Finally, prepare common test data for testing the units.

Complete Technical Design

In this step, estimate the impact of any scope changes that may have occurred along the way and complete any outstanding design work. This effort requires identifying and estimating additional software units. The estimates need to be included in the initial project plan and possibly even reviewed by project stakeholders and approved again by management.

Design Work Units

Review the program architecture developed during technical design and prepare detailed documentation for each programming work unit. It is important to review the technical design before designing any individual work units. Benchmark any likely risk areas to identify and resolve problems, and address potential schedule impacts as soon as possible.

Complete Database Design

Document the logical data views, physical databases or data structures, and data areas used in each programming work unit and make this documentation available to programmers. Build the data structures using the environment or technology tools agreed upon as part of earlier stages.

Review Perform Design

Each analyst conducts a walk-through of the programming unit design with the end users, the application architects, peers, and programming manager and the complete project team. This review step ensures that the design meets the functional and quality requirements of the system, that programmers can understand the requirements, and that the design is technically feasible and will work. The design review may not be a one-time isolated event because it may make sense to conduct different review sessions based on the audience and the purpose of the particular review.

Iterate Detail Design

After the design review stage, it is not uncommon to need one or more repetitive cycles of the preceding steps of the process. This "design and refine" is a common iterative process that allows the project team to get closer and closer to the "real goal" of the system before needing to write a line of code. The traditional "waterfall" method of project management—in which a new phase was not begun until the previous one was complete—never provided for an iteration step. This method is one developed and first used as a result of newer "rapid application development" methodologies (see Chapter 12 for more information on rapid development projects) and object-oriented programming. Today, most project methodologies follow a hybrid of waterfall and iterative processes.

Prepare Common Test Data

Construct a master test database with which to test work units. This database must remain separate from any product database in order to minimize the impact of new systems development and testing from a live, working business environment. Devise a method or a set of programs to update or refresh the test data for testing the unique conditions required for each unit. Prepare test data and document expected results that will fully explore all of the operational conditions that an individual module will face. Prepare user instructions, such as test scenarios or scripts, and possibly sample documents for use in testing the units.

Programming

In this step, the programmers write the code, debug, and deliver tested, executable code for the application. Include any integration of modules that needs to occur in order to complete a logical work unit or application. Write and check the code, allowing programmers to run the first sets of tests during the build process. Run the unit and string tests on logical collections of programs or components. Check the results against the expected results and correct any errors.

Generate and Code Work Units

The process of writing code converts the logical detailed design into the actual physical application run by the computer. This involves writing the application using a high-level programming language or tool, writing intermediate specifications for a code-generation tool, or writing job control statements for a mainframe application. The results are checked and the programmer removes any syntax or execution errors found in this stage.

Prepare Test Data

Prepare sufficient test data sets to test the code fully. This activity will depend heavily on the common test data developed during the Design Phase. The team develops the test data in reference to this plan and prepares and documents expected results.

Perform Code Review

The code review step is conducted by the programmer who wrote the code, the analyst who designed the programming work unit, and possibly by one or two other programmers. There are several reasons for doing a code review. One reason is to ensure that the code accurately reflects the design. Another is to detect defects in the code at an early stage. Also, code reviews that involve peer programmers can be a vital step in assuring overall program quality. Finally, code reviews validate that the code created complies with any coding standards that have been established.

Conduct Unit and String Test

Unit and integration tests yield error-free code that processes the data accurately and reliably, according to specifications. In unit testing, the programmer checks the results of the test against the expected results and corrects any errors detected. String testing verifies the communication between programs or application components and precedes integration testing in the Test Phase. String testing is performed across the host boundary and among all screens or dialogs within a conversation.

▶ Roles

The roles of the participants at this stage have been described in earlier chapters.

Designer
Programmer
Project Management
Technical Architect
Tester

▶ Inputs

Design Document

The Design Document includes and/or references the application architecture, application flow, database design, user interface design, and the workflow diagram. The specific portions of the design document used as inputs during the Construction Phase are the database design or data dictionary, user interface design, and the workflow diagram.

▶ Outputs

Code

Program source, object, and/or executable code, Job Control Language (JCL), data definition language (DDL), HTML, etc., that implement the programming work units.

Programming Work Units

Programming work units are an output of the detailed design and are used as the basis for the development of code.

Programming work units are developed for application programs, special conversion programs, and any special testing aids that may be required. In addition, nonprocedural code is developed for any batch job control, user interface specifications, DDL, etc.

Test Database

The test database is a set of common test data developed to provide quality control for unit testing. The common test data should be modified as needed to reflect unique conditions for specific program work units.

Unit/String Test Results

The actual test results from unit (and string, if applicable) tests should be documented and preserved as part of the system documentation.

▶ Milestones

Code Review Complete

The review of code developed during the Construction Phase has been completed.

String Test Sign-Off

String test sign-off indicates the acceptance of string test results and implies the completion of unit testing.

▶ Tools

The tools for this phase are too numerous and subjective to list. The primary "tools" used by the project team at this point are the specific languages, compilers, and testing tools that are specific to the project environment. More detail on testing tools will be covered in the next chapter.

Test Planning and Preparation

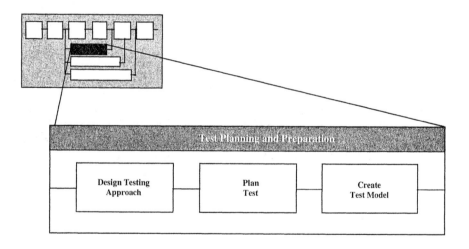

Design Testing Approach	Plan Test	Create Test Model

▶ Purpose

The purpose of the Test Planning and Preparation Phase is to determine the testing required for producing a quality system and ensuring that adequate plans and data exist to conduct the testing. Testing often becomes the critical path activity on the project because rarely is this task planned for until the programs are largely written, and, even when planned for, it is usually underestimated and understaffed. The level of

107

planning described in this section should improve the efficiency of the Testing Phase. The process map above depicts the activities required to complete the Test Planning and Preparation Phase.

▶ Objectives

The key objectives for this phase are as follows:

- Develop a comprehensive plan for the test activities
- Develop a test model that will verify that the system is processing correctly
- Ensure that time and resources required for testing will be available

▶ Activities

Design Testing Approach

The purpose of this activity is to prepare for the testing that takes place. Determine the level (e.g., string, system, integration, user acceptance, etc.) and the type (e.g., stress, regression, performance, etc.) of testing that is appropriate for the application. Finally, ensure that all necessary tools will be available.

These are the types of tests that are typically found in a software project. Not all of these are always used on every project, but one or more are found in most projects.

> **String Test:** String testing verifies the communication between programs or application components and precedes integration testing in the Test Phase. String testing may include function testing, in which each of the program's internal functions are tested.
>
> **Component Test:** The first test of a system in which some or all of the components are tested together. In this test, all

of the program's externals are tested, based on the project specifications.

System Test: A test of an interconnected set of components to check proper functioning and interconnection. System testing usually does not begin until all component testing has been completed. The system test usually tests all major functions of the integrated system, using a typical total systems environment that includes user testing of all external functions and interfaces.

Integration Test: Testing in which software and/or hardware components are combined and tested progressively until the entire system has been integrated.

User Acceptance Test: Tests of external interfaces and dialogs to ensure that user requirements for major functionality have been met.

Stress Test: Testing aimed at investigating the behavior of software or hardware equipment in and out of ordinary operating conditions.

Regression Test: When making improvements to or changes in software, retesting previously tested functions to make sure that adding new features has not introduced new problems. Regression tests are frequently used in the final test of the product, where carefully selected scripts are run as a final verification that the code produced is, indeed, functioning as it should.

Performance Test: Testing of the system using typical user or system resource loads to ensure that the system performs as required.

Black Box: An abstraction of a device or system in which only its externally visible behavior is considered and not its implementation or "inner workings." Functional testing is often referred to as *black box* because this process applies the test data derived from the specified functional requirements without regard to the final program structure.

White Box: Software testing approaches that examine the program structure and derive test data from the program logic. Structural testing is sometimes referred to as *white-box* (or *clear-box*) testing because white boxes are considered opaque and do not really permit visibility into the code.

Plan Test

The test plan must include the specific testing to be performed, the testing approach, test conditions, test schedule, cycle control sheet, test method(s), expected results, and the personnel who will be involved. Generally, a test plan is developed for each test activity, such as string, unit, component, and system testing. The development and testing of both automated and manual test procedures are also defined and specified within the test plan.

Systems and user personnel are extensively involved throughout system testing. This enables end users to become familiar with the new operating procedures in a gradual way.

Create Test Model

A system test model represents a production environment and includes all databases and files. The system test model can be used to test every system modification fully.

▶ Roles

The roles used in this phase are:

Test Analyst
Customer
Designer
Tester(s)

▶ Inputs

The Corporation IT Standards Environment

The *IT Standards Environment* document is used to determine the set of testing tools to be used for the different test stages.

Conversion Plan

The conversion plan specifies the order in which parts of the application will be implemented and the functionality corresponding to each release.

Data Conversion Processes

The data conversion processes document the design of the one-time application required to create the live databases for the system.

Design Document

The design document includes and/or references the application architecture, application flow, database design, user interface design, and the workflow diagram. The specific portions of the design document used as inputs during the Test Planning and Preparation Phase are the application flow and the workflow diagram.

Requirements Specification

The requirements specification includes and/or provides reference to the data model, event model, process model, and quality requirements. The specific descriptions for each of these reside within the analysis phase section of this document.

▶ Outputs

Automated and Manual Test Procedures

All of the automated and manual test procedures are fully tested and debugged.

Test Model

The test model represents the production environment and includes all databases and files.

Test Plan

The test plan defines the testing approach and schedule. The testing approach specifically describes the various levels and types of testing required, who is to perform each level of test, what the objective of the test is, exit criteria for each test, how test data will be created and used, and the resources required. The test plan also contains the test conditions, the cycle control sheet, and the expected results.

▶ Milestones

Test Plan Sign-Off

The test plan sign-off indicates acceptance of the test plan. The test plan sign-off also indicates acceptance of the test model.

▶ Testing Phase

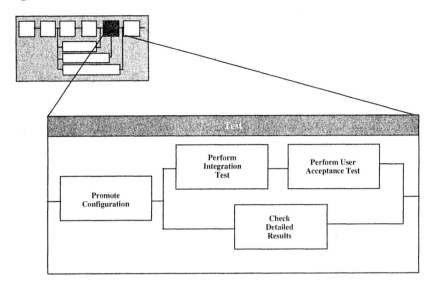

Purpose

Although some testing has been occurring throughout the Construction Phase as programs are being built, this phase refers to a formal phase in which testing and repair are the primary focus. The purpose of the Test Phase is to perform all of the final testing that verifies that the system is ready for rollout. This testing ensures that requirements (both user and quality) are met. The process map above depicts the flow of activities required to complete the Test Phase.

Objectives

The key objectives for this phase are as follows:

- Verify, before conversion, that the new system contains all required functions
- Verify that the functions are performed accurately

- Verify that the system works with all interfacing systems
- Verify that the new system meets quality and/or standards requirements

Activities

Promote Configuration

The promotion process involves the linking of program units, database structures, and any other executable components into the completed application. This process includes building the application, performing the installation, then verifying that the installation was performed correctly.

Perform Integration Test

The integration test verifies the accuracy of the communication among all programs in the new system and between the new system and all of the external interfaces. The integration test must also prove that the new system performs according to the functional specifications and functions effectively in the operating environment without adversely affecting other systems.

Perform User Acceptance Test

The user acceptance test simulates the actual working conditions of the new system, including the user manuals and procedures. Extensive user involvement in this stage of testing provides the user with invaluable training in operating the new system. It also benefits the programmer or designer to see the user experience with the new programs. This joint involvement encourages the user and operations personnel to approve the system conversion.

Check Detailed Results

The project manager and the team members must check the detailed testing results of each cycle in a uniform way. Rechecking the detail in subsequent test cycles verifies the proper performance of each function under normal and abnormal conditions. This becomes especially critical in the regression testing phase, where the same sections of code are tested and retested against the data sets until all details have been verified to be functioning and error free.

Roles

The roles used in this phase include:

Tester(s)

User

Inputs

Automated and Manual Test Procedures

All of the automated and manual test procedures should be fully unit tested and debugged by the programmer or tester before they enter into the formal Test Phase. If users are to be involved in any of this testing, their test scripts and documentation must be available and tested, as well.

Code

Program source, object, and executable code, JCL, DDL, etc., that implement the work unit specifications.

Test Model

The test model represents the production environment and includes all databases, data sources, and files.

Test Plan

The test plan includes the testing approach, schedule, resources, and scripts. The testing approach specifically addresses the various levels and types of testing required, who is to perform each level of test, what the objective of the test is, exit criteria for each test, how test data will be created and used, and the resources required. The test plan also contains the test conditions, the cycle control sheet, and the expected results. Any error-tracking databases or tracking sheets that are being used in the testing process should be included in the test plan.

User Documentation

The documents and procedures that the end users follow when they are using the system must be available at this time. User documentation may be "tested" in this phase as well, because errors that are discovered in testing can often be documentation errors or misunderstandings that cause the users to work with the system in a way that is not expected. Errors in documentation need to be tracked, repaired, and followed up on in the same way as program errors.

Outputs

Test Results

These are the results of comparing test output to expected results. The results are evidence that all the planned cycles have run successfully and that all outstanding issues are resolved.

Milestones

Conversion Readiness Sign-Off

The sponsor, the end users, and the IS department all agree to convert the system, phasing out old procedures, programs, data, and equipment. This sign-off is obtained just before conversion, while it is not too late to call it off or postpone the conversion.

The successful completion of all levels of test is one of several requirements for conversion sign-off. The other requirements are the completion of the rollout planning and preparation activities and the completion of the user procedures development and user training activities.

▶ Tools

There are numerous tools used in this phase to create the necessary deliverables, as well as any intermediate work documents. Some of these deliverables will require, or at least justify, specialized tools, whereas others will make use of standard tools, such as word processing software, presentation tools, and spreadsheets.

Testing Tools: Testing tools are very specific to the types of environments, programs, and the types of testing to be performed on them. Popular tools for Windows-based and web-based environments include product suites by Mercury Interactive, Intersolve, QES, McCabe and Associates, Pure/Atria (acquired by Rational Software) and Platinum (Unix-based or networking tools include Applied Computer Technology [ACT], International Software Automation, Inc. (ISA), and Software Research Inc).

Bug Tracking Databases: Another important aspect of the testing process is the tool and process used to identify, categorize, log, and track the resolution of bugs found. Many project teams prefer to create their own bug database, but there are a number of good commercial products available in the market. Archimedes™, QADB (which is a free, web-based tracking tool), and Soffront Software, makers of Track™.

Other important tools to have in the Construction/Testing Phase are change management tools/databases and source code control systems that help control environments in which several programmers may be working with multiple versions of code at the same time. Without robust change management or source control management practices in use, it is easy to overwrite or undo changes that have been made by someone else, which results in significant lost time and productivity.

▶ Preparation Phase

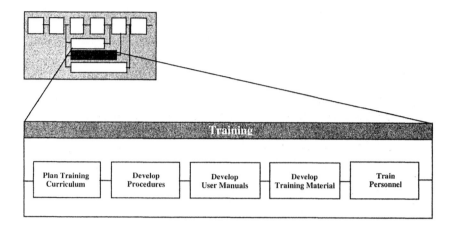

Purpose

The purpose of the Preparation Phase is to create all required end user procedures, documentation, or manuals and to develop and provide user training on the new system. Computer operations and production support procedures are also developed at this time. The end users of the new system are then trained according to the training curriculum. The process map above depicts the high-level activities required to complete the Preparation Phase.

Objectives

The key objectives for this phase are as follows:

- Plan for and ensure that all aspects of the system are documented in the form of user procedures or manuals and that these procedures are then collated into user manuals.
- Finalize the format of input documents and output forms.
- Draw on the user manuals and procedures for developing training manuals, pilot-test them for effectiveness, and train the personnel who will use the system, and incorporate feedback into the training program.

Activities

Plan Training Curriculum

Determine who needs to be trained on the new system, the skill sets required, and how personnel are to be trained. Develop a training schedule that includes time and cost estimates for developing curriculum, as well as for delivering training. When developing the cost estimates, a broad-thinking project manager will include not only time/ cost estimates for project staff required to develop and deliver the training, but will be conscious of indirect costs incurred by the project due to lack of productivity by end users, as a result of having them away from their normal jobs while they attend training. This should be represented in training estimates in some fashion.

Develop Procedures

The project manager and the team develop user procedures for the performance, security, control, and computer operation functions that support the system. The team finalizes the design of all preprinted input documents, special stationery, and preprinted output forms. The team also designs templates for Internet word processing, spreadsheet, and electronic mail system components.

The operations instructions contain instructions to help operations and helpdesk personnel. Specific operating instructions are usually identified and developed for each application system. These manuals will combine the new procedures with those already in place for existing application systems.

Develop and complete the user procedures and operations instructions early so that they can be used during the programming, system test, and conversion.

Develop User Manuals

Combine all the detailed user, security, and control procedures into the user manuals. If a packaged system is used, the documentation supplied by the vendor may be incorporated into the user manuals or may serve as a self-contained manual. Key members of the user team should review the user manuals under development. This helps to ensure that the documentation is readable and accurately reflects the business processes performed. Code testers should also review documentation for accuracy against the actual programs that have been developed.

Develop Training Material

Using input from the user manuals and procedures, develop the required training materials, including visual aids, instructor guides, and self-study materials. Conduct a pilot test or walk-through of the training sessions and materials to determine their effectiveness. This is an ideal time to "train the trainer" if some key project staff will be assisting in propagating the training to other members of the organization.

Train Personnel

Provide training to personnel and ensure completion of the training before conducting the user assurance checks and system conversion. This has two benefits: It allows the user personnel to become significantly involved in both tasks, and it provides feedback from the participants and instructors to help the project team determine the success of the training.

Roles

The roles used in this phase include:

Human Factors
Technical Writer
Trainer
User

Inputs

Design Document

The design document includes and/or references the application architecture, application flow, database design, user interface design, and the workflow diagram. The specific portions of the design document used as inputs during the training phase are the user interface design and the workflow diagram.

User Documentation Outline

The user documentation outline records the manual procedures to be developed and how they will be organized.

User Documentation Standards

If any standards documents have been created as part of the overall project standards, these documents will need to be available and finalized prior to beginning drafts of any documentation or training.

Outputs

Operations Instructions

Operations instructions include manuals, installation procedures, and instructions for the new system to be used by the application control center, production support, helpdesk, etc.

Training Curriculum

The training curriculum specifies the target user and operations personnel to be trained, the required courses by category of personnel, and the strategy for each course (content, delivery mechanism). A plan to continue training new users after implementation and rollout should be documented and included in the curriculum.

Training Materials

Training materials in the form of computer-based training (CBT), self-study or instructor-led courses, on-line tutorials, and other materials are prepared for two types of audiences: end users of the current system who will convert to using the new system at the time of project rollout and continuing training for new end users who join the departments after the system has been implemented. The materials and training approach for the two may be different because users who are trained at the time of initial system rollout may have relearning to do as a result of moving from an "old" system to this new one. Users who join the department or begin working with the business processes well after implementation may not have any unlearning to do; instead, they are working on this new system "fresh" and need training only on the new system's procedures without having to be "untrained" on the old.

User Documentation

Whether in the form of user manuals or an on-line help facility containing field definitions, application definitions, and error handling to guide end users, this documentation helps end users to use the system correctly and provides them a reference for future assistance. It includes both routine tasks (in a task-oriented user guide) and complete reference materials (in the reference manual). Some of the user documentation may be in the form of forms and supplies, referring both to the master copies of all preprinted input forms and to the actual forms and supplies.

Milestones

Preparation Plan Sign-Off

The preparation phase documents the training needs of the organization and relates them to the available training courses through a schedule. Sign-off of this plan indicates acceptance of the plan and commits to funding the execution of the training.

User Procedures Sign-Off

The completed user procedures and documentation must be approved by representatives of the customer and end user community, as well as the development and testing groups to confirm that the procedures are understandable by end users, that they meet their requirements, and that they are procedurally correct and technically accurate for the new system.

Conversion Readiness Sign-Off

The sponsor, the end users, and the IT department all agree to implement the system, phasing out old procedures, programs, data, and equipment as necessary. This sign-off is obtained just before implementation, while it is not too late to call off or postpone the implementation.

The completion of the user procedures development and user training activities are two of several requirements for implementation sign-off. The other requirements are completion of the roll-out planning and preparation activities (discussed in the next chapter) and successful completion of all levels of testing.

Rollout Planning and Implementation Phase

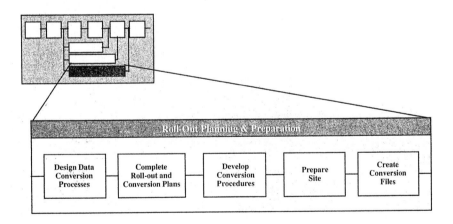

▶ Purpose

The purpose of the Rollout Planning and Preparation Phase is to begin all preparation activities necessary for rolling out the new system to the end users and to the production environment. This phase is performed to ensure that the rollout of the new system will proceed smoothly and on schedule. The process map above depicts the high-level activities required for completing the Rollout Planning and Implementation Phase.

▶ Objectives

The key objectives for this phase are as follows:

- Ensure that it is possible to migrate from the current to the new system, as applicable
- Create the basis for estimating any one-time migration efforts
- Complete a comprehensive plan for any necessary conversion activities
- Prepare the end users and the sites for the rollout of the system

▶ Activities

Design Data Conversion Processes

The project team ensures that all data required by the system is available. The team also develops contingency plans that address the possibility that data is not ready on implementation day.

The project team designs the overall data conversion flow and the data conversion programs, as needed. For new systems that are not replacing any existing systems, data conversion may not be required because the system will likely be starting with fresh information. Data conversion techniques and schedules should be reviewed by all key members of the project team, including the user subject matter experts, because they are used to working with the existing data and can help to verify that the data to be converted is being handled in an appropriate manner.

Complete Rollout and Conversion Plans

The conversion plan identifies the overall approach for the conversion of the entire system or system upgrade, from the old configuration to the new. The rollout plan confirms the order in which sites will be converted and determines their scheduling dependencies. The plans must assign responsibilities to specific individuals, assess the level of effort required, and identify the time frame for performing each work step.

Develop Conversion Procedures

The conversion procedures are the main tools used to perform the work steps defined in the conversion plan. Most of the procedures deal with the creation, update, and maintenance of files and databases. Other significant conversion procedures relate to control, backup, contingencies, and deployment of the application at various sites. The published conversion procedures provide the basis for scheduling, training, and coordinating the conversion effort.

Prepare Site

The project team must plan for and estimate the cost of any physical facilities construction that may be associated with the conversion. Also, any capital or other acquisitions, such as computer hardware or software, need to be planned, and shipment and installation time should be accounted for. The plan should include a schedule of completion dates and responsibilities for all tasks related to conversion preparation so that the project manager can monitor the progress of the work.

Create Conversion Files

The project team gathers the data needed for conversion from existing databases and other sources. For new systems, the database contains only master and reference tables and data. Transaction files are generated in day-to-day operation of the new system. Systems converted in their entirety may have their transaction data converted as individual records or as summary data, in addition to reference information. In any case, it is critical to ensure that the data has been accurately and completely transcribed from its original format into the format required by the new system.

▶ Roles

The roles used in this phase include:

Conversion test team: A specialized team whose primary responsibility is to verify the accuracy and completeness of converted data in the new system.

Customer or client: The end user of their system.

▶ Inputs

Design Document

The design document includes and/or references the application architecture, application flow, database design, user interface design, and the workflow diagram. The specific portions of the design document used as inputs during the Rollout Planning and Preparation Phase are the application architecture and the database design.

Current System Descriptions

Descriptions of the current system are used to help define any physical changes to the existing infrastructure that need to be accomplished as a part of the conversion process.

▶ Outputs

Conversion Plan

The conversion plan documents the considerations and requirements for converting a specific site from the old system to the new.

Converted Data

Converted data are data that was present in the previous system that is converted and reformatted for use in the new system.

Data Conversion Processes

The data conversion processes document the design of the one-time application required to create the live databases for the system.

Rollout Plan

The rollout plan defines the process and the schedule for rolling out the overall system. It states which sites need to be converted, in what order, and the timing and dependencies of the conversions.

▶ Milestones

Conversion Readiness Sign-Off

The sponsor, the end users, and the IT department all agree to convert the system, phasing out old procedures, programs, data, and equipment. This sign-off is obtained just before beginning conversion, while it is not too late to call off or postpone the conversion.

The completion of the rollout planning and preparation activities and outputs are two of several requirements for conversion sign-off. The other requirements are the successful completion of user procedures development, user training, and successful completion of all levels of test.

▶ Rollout

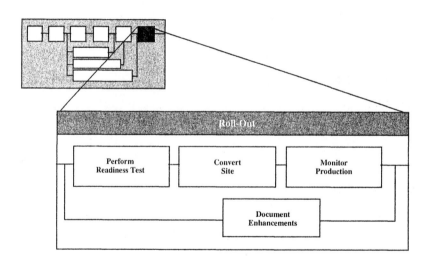

Purpose

The purpose of the Rollout Phase is to install the new system into the production environment, complete the conversion processes, and release the system for use by its customers and end users. Rollout also incorporates brief periods of end user and system assurance checks to ensure successful conversion. The process map above depicts the high-level activities required to complete the Rollout Phase.

Objectives

The key objectives for this phase are as follows:

- Convert to the new or modified system
- Provide an environment that will ensure the continued success of the system

Activities

Perform Readiness Check

The operational readiness and user assurance checks help to mitigate the risks associated with conversion. The operational readiness check will ensure that the physical environment is correct and will verify that the operations architecture will support the configuration. The user assurance check familiarizes the end users with the functionality of the new system in a controlled environment. This helps to achieve user buy-in by providing them an environment in which to become comfortable with the system, without the fear of affecting live production data. These checks also confirm that user personnel have been trained properly.

Convert System

Convert the application from the old system to the new, following the plans and materials that were previously developed. The conversion includes distributing new materials and documentation and implementing the new automated and manual procedures.

Implementing the new programs and distributing the procedures does not, however, complete the conversion. The new system must be a continuing part of the business and compatible with the existing operating environment. Remove all old system manuals and automated procedures from the production environment and assure that obsolete tasks are discontinued.

Monitor Production

The project team members evaluate the new system to identify potential areas for improvement. They compare the number of operating personnel actually required to the original estimates. They observe operating environment procedures and enhance the procedures as necessary to improve workflow.

Document Potential Enhancements

During the conversion, personnel using the system identify corrections and improvements for the system. Some of these are critical and require immediate implementation, whereas others can be considered for implementation in a subsequent project.

Roles

The roles used in this phase include:

Conversion Team

Project Management

Inputs

Conversion Plan

The conversion plan documents site conversion considerations, schedule, and requirements for a specific system.

Operations Instructions

Operations instructions include manuals and installation procedures for the new system to be used by the application control center, production support, helpdesk, etc.

Rollout Plan

The rollout plan defines the overall system rollout process and schedule. It states which sites will be converted, in what order, and shows the timing and dependencies of the conversions. This plan also includes detailed schedules for construction, equipment and software installation, and delivery of supplies.

End User Documentation

Whether in the form of user manuals or an on-line help facility containing field definitions, application definitions, and error handling to guide end users, the user documentation helps end users to use the system correctly. It includes both routine tasks (in a task-oriented user guide) and complete reference materials (in the reference manual). Some of the documentation may be in the form of forms and supplies, referring both to the master copies of all preprinted input forms and to the actual forms and supplies.

Outputs

Change Requests

A change request formally documents any problem or enhancement to be addressed by the project or production systems support.

Postconversion Review Document

The postconversion review documents the successful conversion of the system. It specifies the scope of the conversion, release identification, any conversion-related information, and any problems encountered during the conversion (with dispositions).

Milestones

Postconversion Review Sign-Off

The postconversion review report is approved by the conversion team, as well as by the end user group, to show that the system was successfully converted and that any conversion-related problems were resolved.

Part 4

Project Management Techniques

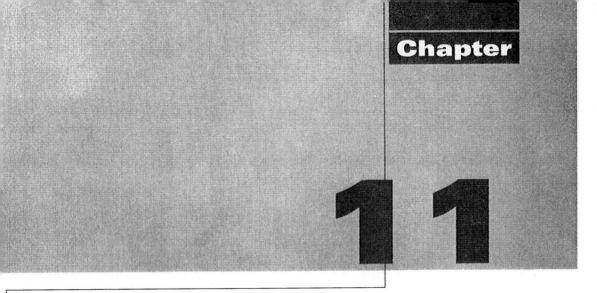

Project Management Methodologies

If you don't know where you are going—any path will take you there.

Ancient Sioux Indian Proverb

▶ Introduction

The tools and techniques that we have traditionally used in new application development have been only partially successful, and the developers are still experiencing significant problems. We are still facing poor software quality, large application development backlogs, missed deadlines, budget overruns, poor project management and estimation, and an unacceptable level of cancelled projects.

Many IT managers have thrown up their arms and all but given up and surrendered. Rather than surrender, IT organizations should start evaluating maturing methodologies and related tools for project planning to make projects more productive. Corporations should embrace and implement integrated methodologies that are now widely available but little used or even understood.

Despite its long-winded name, a methodology is a very useful tool in the IT project management arsenal. In the early 1970s, when methodologies first became known, critics unkindly said that these tools were "short on methods, long on 'ologies.'" There may have been some basis for truth in that statement; however, in the fast cycle time of the late 1990s and early 2000s, this is no longer the case because methodologies have matured and become widely accepted.

Methodologies are not just a tool for the IT industry; they have been successfully used by other professions in fields such as:

- Engineering—electrical, mechanical, construction
- Medical—nursing, pathology, pharmacology, gerontology
- General Research—collecting and analyzing data, statistics
- Space—developing space systems, navigation, flight telemetry
- Military—ordnance, logistics, surveillance
- Legal—teaching of law
- Manufacturing—developing and deploying factory systems
- Teaching—learning approaches

IT managers should ask themselves some crucial questions on how to address the fast cycle times that we live in and what tools, methods, and techniques should be used. More than ever, we need effective tools that can help us to be more productive.

There are fundamental questions that should be asked by every corporation interested in increasing the success and efficiency of their project management endeavors:

1. What are the dominant trends in application development that are available to my organization that will increase productivity significantly, that is, 30% or more?
2. What mature, proven methodologies, project management tools, and repeatable processes are available to meet this goal?
3. What are the benefits of a methodology to my organization?
4. How do I go about selecting and implementing a methodology?
5. How can I convince my senior management that this is not another gimmick, buzz word, or "silver bullet?"
6. How can I produce metrics and definitive data on productivity?
7. Will my end users and project team be able to use a methodology?
8. What training do I need to be successful?

▶ What Is a Methodology, and Why Use One?

We define a *methodology* as a set of *repeatable processes* with project-specific methods, rules, and guidelines for building quality application systems that are manageable and deliver value to the organization.

The key phrase here is "repeatable process"—doing projects the same way. To think of this another way, a methodology is a road map to get you to where you want to be. A methodology delivers value and productivity to organizations by describing a repeatable set of processes and procedures for building systems.

Methodologies are converging with project management techniques, process management techniques, and others to provide a delivery vehicle for addressing many of today's application development problems.

▶ Methodology Structures

Most methodologies consist of four basic components:

1. Guidelines—Specific steps necessary for successful application development. Guidelines contain advice and recommendations on how to proceed.

2. Techniques—The detailed process descriptions that support the activities throughout the entire software development lifecycle (SDLC). Techniques provide assistance for completing the deliverables

3. Tools—Particularly, project management tools integrated with the methodology that draws on past project experiences. Most methodologies are independent of the primary application development software. This means that it can be used with any language, from legacy COBOL systems that are 30 years old to fourth-generation languages (4GLs), CASE tools, to object-oriented systems.

4. Templates—Reusable documents and checklists that give advice and assistance.

A methodology should also be able to furnish multiple different project routes to provide support for the increasingly complex structure of today's IS systems. Examples or different routes or techniques include:

- Client/server application
- Software package selection
- Rapid application development
- Small projects
- Host-based development
- Information or strategic planning
- Legacy systems development
- Interfacing and bridging of systems
- Infrastructure planning
- Migration planning
- Iterative and prototyping development
- Intranet and collaborative projects
- Internet-based projects

▶ Why Use a Methodology?

There are major benefits and significant productivity gains to be made by using a standard approach or a methodology for the application development process. Project management benefits include the following:

1. Management can protect its investment by ensuring that the project's supports are well defined and likely to succeed. Methodologies frequently have a deliverable in the form of a business case—a report that defines the economics, benefits, costs, resources needed, and so on. This ensures that the project is oriented toward the company's business needs. To provide such guidance, the business case is updated throughout the project lifecycle to reflect changes that affect the ongoing and one-time costs and benefits of the new system.

2. Management and users know in advance what they can expect from each project. As each unit of work—be it a phase, a seg-

ment, or a task—is completed, certain standard deliverables and work products are developed that explain the work accomplished and the decisions reached. These work products are used as input for the following unit of work and for helping management to ensure that all work has been properly completed. Predefined sign-off points, sometimes called *milestones*, allow management and users to give their approval and to ensure that the project's goals are met.

3. Results are of high quality. Quality requirements and verification are integral parts of any good methodology. The methodology should provide checklists and templates to ensure that quality expectations are being met. These work products help to define how well the system operates and meets the original project requirements and focuses on the system's usability, maintainability, flexibility, and reliability, enabling the development team to design the necessary quality attributes into the system.

    Quality assurance reviews or audits give management an independent assessment of the caliber of work done. These reviews ensure that the prescribed development process is being followed; that risks are identified, communicated, and managed; and that the project works to meet its scope and objectives. In general, applications that are constructed with a methodology have higher quality than do those not utilizing them.

4. Surprises, such as cost overruns, scope changes, late implementation, and other risks, can be minimized. Methodologies have risk assessment and control procedures to mitigate project risks. Project plans include specific start and completion dates for the work performed during a project. They provide guidelines for conducting a project and make it easy to track progress and highlight potential delays or overruns in advance so that corrective action can be taken. Surprises are not acceptable and less likely when using a methodology.

5. The status of all projects is readily accessible. Good methodologies frequently have project management software embedded or integrated into the products. This allows the project team members to prepare time reports that include estimated time to complete each assigned activity. Using these time reports and the project's work program or plan, the project manager can accurately assess the status of the project. The project manager's

assessments are documented in regular (weekly or biweekly) progress reports to senior management.

6. Productivity is increased. Organizations that embrace methodologies generally realize significant increases in the productivity of application development. This is because there is a set of guidelines under which to operate; there is no "figuring it out or making it up as you go," which tends to consume a lot of project management and project team cycles.

7. Communication is improved. A methodology sets standards that everyone can follow. It sets clear and agreed-upon expectations. It can specify a framework of what tasks are to be performed, when to perform them, the sequence required, how to perform them, and how to communicate and manage the process.

Methodologies are frequently integrated within project management software tools and process management techniques to provide a valuable delivery vehicle.

▶ Author's Prediction

Consistent and repeated use of a methodology can provide the majority of organizations with an application development and project management productivity improvement at a *minimum* level of at least 30%. Past experience has shown that the most productive projects of all, in general, are those using 4GLs or other code-type generators in conjunction with a moderately rigid methodology. Users of this approach have documented productivity increases of as much as 70%.

Research organizations such as the Gartner Group, Meta, the Giga Information Group, and others indicate that as much as 70% of all corporations do not use a standard methodology. They continue to use unstructured methods or no methods at all. This is a serious concern and shows how little methodology use is accepted, but major increases in application development productivity await those corporations that do embrace a methodology.

▶ What Are the Products?

Table 11-1 contains a list of some of the major players in the methodology product marketplace.

Table 11-1 A Sample List of Methodology Products

Product	Vendor
Process Engineer	Platinum, Inc.
SUMMIT	Price Waterhouse Coopers
Map	Protellicess
METHOD/1	Andersen Consulting
Surveyor	Bachman
Key-Advise	Sterling Software
Navigator	Ernst & Young
Architect	JMC, Inc.
SE/Companion	SECA, Inc.

Some of these methodologies are commercially available as products. Others "come with" the consulting services that the particular vendor supplies and are not independently available. Still other methodologies are included as an underlying, selectable part of project management tools, such as those available from ABT Corporation.

▶ A Case in Point

The Kroger Co. is the largest retail food company in the United States, as measured by total annual sales. Kroger was founded in 1883 by Barney Kroger in Cincinnati, Ohio, where its headquarters remain today. Its mission is to continue to be a leader in the distribution and merchandising of food; pharmaceutical, health, and personal care items; seasonal merchandise and related products; and, more recently, diversified services such as insurance and other financial services.

Kroger has come a long way since Barney's first grocery store. At the end of 1997, it operated 1,392 food stores under seven names across 24 states and 816 convenience stores under six logos in 15 states. Food stores are its primary business and account for over 93% of total company sales. Convenience stores and 36 manufacturing facilities contribute the remainder of total sales. Total number of employees is over 170,000.

To achieve this growth, Kroger has earned a track record of innovation in both its national store facilities and information systems. The senior IT management made a decision to implement a methodology and set about training every member of the 250-person IT department, from the junior trainees to its senior managers.

Kroger's objectives in using a methodology were as follows:

- Obtain a predictable, repeatable process that is structured, yet flexible, and has multiple development routes.

- Provide a standard way to plan, estimate, and schedule projects.

- Capture analysis and design deliverables in a common repository for storing project documentation and promoting the use of standards.

Since then, major increases in productivity have been realized, higher-quality systems have been delivered, all of this in a climate of continuous change and complexity. Kroger's IT Director, Larry Braun, sums up its experiences:

> *"With the Methodology, our developers can produce more consistent results than they could before and in less time. The methodology is more than a development process. It is a part of the Kroger culture."*

Since using this methodology, Kroger has been able to sustain some key benefits, namely:

- All major systems have been delivered on schedule.

- Systems designs and enhancements are done faster, with predictable, repeatable results.

- Project estimates and schedules accurately reflect real budget and project duration.

- Developers communicate more effectively through a common set of processes and tools.

▶ Conclusions

Methodologies have been among the most discussed and least implemented of all approaches to improving software quality and productivity in an IT organization. To the best of this author's knowledge, these arguments have been going on now for over 25 years. The concept behind the use of a methodology is so simple as to hardly require explanation: Do not reinvent that which has already been built; construct *new* systems and functions from the same building blocks used to build systems and functions already tested and proven in actual use. Use repeatable processes wherever possible while improving where possible. Comparisons to modern manufacturing methods are obvious and correct, and it is clear that systematic, repeatable processes are essential both to the "software factory" and to technical methods (such as object-oriented design) for creating the software factory approach.

Why then do so few IT organizations have ongoing, successful methodology programs? This author remains baffled for a complete and satisfactory answer.

An analogy to a regular exercise program is relevant here. We all know that exercise is good for us. The benefits are obvious, visible, healthy, well documented and understood, not very long in coming, and there are few, if any, good reasons to avoid it. However, many people avoid it nevertheless. Some avoid it altogether because it involves:

1. A change in routine

2. Effort and discipline

3. Some initial pain, no matter how small

Methodology implementation is almost like exercise, the hardest thing is to *get started and keep it up*. No pain—no gain.

▶ Suggested Readings

Avison, D.E. and Fitzgerald, G. *Information Systems Development: Methodologies, Techniques and Tools*. Books Britain, 1995.

Martin, James and Leben, Joe. *Strategic Information Planning Methodologies*. Prentice Hall, 1984.

Olle, T. William. *Information Systems Methodologies: A Framework for Understanding*. John Wiley & Sons, 1994.

Purba, Sanjiv. *How to Manage a Successful Software Project: Methodologies, Techniques, Tools*. John Wiley & Sons, 1995.

Managing Rapid Application Development

▶ Introduction

Flexibility, speed, and change are becoming standard characteristics of successful organizations in the new millennium and beyond. The need for flexibility and change extends through every organization—local to global—and to its information systems groups in terms of reduced development times, support for smaller project teams, and control of development costs. Rapid Application Development (RAD) is an approach that provides a repeatable process that addresses these issues.

Rapid development integrates the best practices of project management techniques, development techniques, users, and tools to build quality application systems in a fixed time frame to deliver business value. Rapid application development combines teams working in a highly structured and motivated environment. A RAD team consists of between three and seven people, all focused on creating a specific application from a prioritized and fixed set of requirements.

Rapid denotes speed and is the watchword of the new millennium. Management and end users think only in speed terms, with questions such as:

- When is the next release?
- When can I get the changes I asked for?
- When can I get the new reports?

Corporations that are not moving quickly will be overtaken by their competitors. As one CIO puts it, "speed kills the competition." It is with this background that the need for RAD has evolved.

▶ RAD Concepts

Rapid Application Development is a highly concentrated process or methodology in which the requirements of projects are fed into a process of speedy development, using an iterative or repetitive technique. The application is developed within a fixed time frame, normally 30, 60, or perhaps even 90 days. Anything over 90 days is not considered to be rapid. The successive development of the application leads to a system that can be used in production and rolled out to end users.

Not all projects are suitable for rapid development. and project managers should use care and good judgment in selecting projects for RAD. There is further discussion on this topic later in this chapter.

RAD is a relatively recent technique, developed in the last 10 years. Its origins are obscure, but many promote it as having been born at DuPont, the U.S.-based chemical manufacturer. In 1990, author James Martin wrote an important book, *Rapid Application Development*, published by McGraw Hill. Many IT people claim that RAD is simply a faster version of joint application development (JAD), an accepted technique that has been valuable for many years. There may be some truth in that statement.

▶ Objectives and Benefits of RAD

Objectives

RAD has a specific set of objectives, namely:

- To develop quality applications in a specific and rapid time-frame—days or weeks, rather than the months and years typically experienced using conventional techniques.
- To provide an environment where end-user involvement is paramount. RAD will not be successful without total end-user involvement.
- To achieve rapid development using highly trained and motivated resources in a structured team environment.

Benefits

RAD offers significant benefits to IT organizations that embrace it and to the end-user community that will use the systems created with it. RAD draws upon the benefits of using existing technology, installed and operational architectures, an integrated development environment, and extremely focused user involvement in order to yield these benefits. They include the following:

- Dramatically shorter application development lifecycles, as indicated above; weeks and days are not uncommon expectations.
- Significant reductions in the cost of application development.
- Increases in software quality—speed does not mean poor results.
- Increases in staff productivity—IT staff does more with less.
- Much easier maintenance of applications.

▶ The RAD Lifecycle

The normal RAD lifecycle consists of four basic phases:

1. Project Management—a continuous and ongoing process. Managing the requirements or scope is an important factor in RAD project management, application development, and implementation. It involves problem solving, making decisions, and working with end users. RAD is only a project technique and must be managed using the same approaches described in this book.

2. Requirements—the system is defined and agreed to prior to development. Some project managers use a RAD technique called *rapid requirements definition* (RRD) to drive out the requirements and obtain agreement quickly. Others prefer to use the more traditional JAD techniques.

3. Application Development—the product is constructed with several iterations or incremental delivery. Prototyping may also be used, where developers provide a "show-and-see" approach. Testing is rolled into this phase and is considered to be a vital part of the process.

4. Implementation and Rollout—the final system is put to use and handed over to the end users. Training and support are also addressed during this phase to ensure that a quality system is delivered.

An optional fifth phase of maintenance is sometimes defined when ongoing application development is a requirement. However, this is normally outside of the agreed time frame and not subject to the time constraints of RAD development. Figure 12–1 illustrates the flow of work.

▶ RAD Project Management Factors

During project planning, project managers need to review, in detail, the various components when considering whether RAD should be the selected technique to use for application development. A general discussion of these factors and benefits follows.

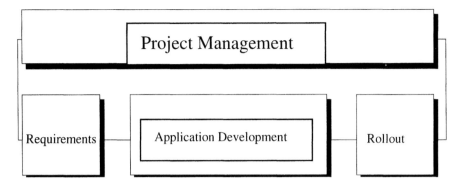

Figure 12–1   A Simple RAD Lifecycle

Shorter Duration

The principle purpose of RAD is to develop applications within a much shorter time frame than with traditional application development methods. Typically, the duration of RAD projects is specified at the project planning phase. Project managers will agree with senior management, the project sponsor, and the end users that the project must be developed in 30, 60, or 90 days. This sets the tone for development and creates a sense of urgency for the project team. This means that there is little room for indecision or lack of agreement. Project managers are often called upon to make rapid decisions.

Empowered End Users

RAD is very popular with the end-user community. When done well, end users see results more quickly than with normal legacy development and are much happier. However, part of RAD's success relies on the total commitment of the end users to the project. End users are there to define the project's requirements. They also guide the application's design and determine the feasibility of the application's rollout. The role of the end users on the project may change throughout the project, such as designing, developing, and involving them in testing and implementation. RAD will need a project sponsor who will champion the project and empower the end users to set priorities and resolve design issues among themselves, to improve communications, and to make decisions. End users who are assertive and aggressive often thrive in the RAD environment. It is not for the faint-hearted or for people who cannot make decisions quickly. End users must be involved on a full-time basis (40 hours per week) for the entire project. Anything else places a successful outcome at risk.

Use of Existing Architectures and Technology

RAD is not suitable for projects that may require new or emerging technology, such as new programming languages, new network designs, new architectures, or other innovative technology. *Technical innovation* is defined as the introduction of new platforms, such as hardware, systems software, database management systems, or networks new to the industry or unproven within the corporation.

Project managers will be aware of the risk that will be present using this approach. RAD makes use of existing platforms that are proven, stable, and reliable. This means using hardware that is already in use, as well as proven software and DBMS systems. There is no room for experimentation with RAD—there simply is no time. It is also a very good idea to reuse code, templates, and design models wherever appropriate. Remember that it is all about speed—delivering quality results quickly.

Proven Methodology

A methodology is a very useful tool in RAD development; it will define the processes and activities that the team will follow in the creation of the application system. The development environment includes a methodology to ensure integration with the other components of the RAD environment. Examples include Process Engineer by Platinum, Andersen Consulting's METHOD/1, Ernst & Young's Navigator, or the SUMMIT products by Price Waterhouse Coopers. When selecting a methodology, it is important to ensure that the products have a RAD path or template. See Chapter 11 for more discussion on the value of methodologies.

A Highly Motivated Team

RAD requires the skill of a highly motivated and energized project team. Project managers must be very careful in selecting team members. There is no time for egos, academics, or people who do not want to work. Team members must be able to sustain pressure and deadlines and to deliver results. Experienced project team members who are respected by end users are frequently the best people to have on the team. There is no time for learning curves on RAD projects, and project team members must immediately set about delivering the agreed project plan. Project managers should provide incentives or bonuses for quality delivery of the project. Appropriate incentives, such as completion bonuses, awards, dinners, or other forms of recognition should be established for success. People make RAD successful. The qualities and individual skills necessary for successful RAD team members are detailed later in this chapter.

Application Complexity

RAD is not suitable for applications that have a high degree of functional complexity or that have high transaction throughput. These systems normally require much longer development time frames and should be avoided. Rapid development provides minimal treatment of performance. The use of an established and reliable architecture should provide an acceptable level of performance. In systems where performance is a significant requirement, a traditional development methodology approach should be used. Batch systems should also be avoided. RAD is not a good technique for developing batch systems. The time constraints imposed on a RAD project cannot support the resolution of detailed technical issues.

The Internet

The Internet or, more specifically, the World Wide Web, has brought a new dimension to RAD development. It enables remote teams to communicate when they are not in the same location. End users can search and find information, specs, research products, templates, use standards, and more. The Internet is a fast place to do business, and there is a wealth of data to be mined.

▶ The Roles of the RAD Team Members

The RAD team is the very heart of the RAD process, and the selection and inclusion of individuals is critical to the overall success of a RAD project. The team consists of a mixture of skills and is comprised of:

- The RAD facilitator or session leader
- A management sponsor
- Information specialists
- End users
- A scribe
- Specialists
- Observers

The RAD Facilitator

The RAD facilitator is the key person in the team and is responsible for planning, executing, and managing the project. Choosing a facilitator is the first important step. He or she should be a respected, skillful leader with a good reputation within the organization. RAD facilitator skills do not happen by chance, and the skills may have to be learned. RAD experience is also necessary. It is not a position to be reached lightly and not for the faint-hearted. Choosing a poor RAD facilitator may mean the difference between a good project and a failed one.

It is essential that the facilitator be given the authority and the responsibility necessary to lead the team. He or she will work closely with the management sponsor to achieve the objectives of the RAD project. The facilitator will know how to handle people to obtain the best results from them. The box below summarizes the profile.

TITLE:	RAD FACILITATOR
ROLE:	Controls and manages the RAD project
QUALITIES:	Leadership Management skills Respected manager within the organization Good people skills Resourcefulness Ability to get results
NO. REQUIRED:	1
EXAMPLES:	Project manager DP manager End user manager

The Management Sponsor

For any computer project to succeed, the backing of management is required. It is very important for the RAD team to have a management sponsor. This person may be a divisional head or manager of the business area that the RAD project is addressing.

The sponsor does not have to participate in every RAD session. It might be advisable for the sponsor to attend the first and perhaps the final RAD session to review the results and to make comments. The sponsor should be available throughout the period of RAD development to solve any serious problems or issues that may arise. The RAD facilitator will work closely with the management sponsor and will be kept fully briefed on progress. The sponsor can be from the end-user community but may likely be the head of data processing. The box below summarizes this role.

TITLE:	MANAGEMENT SPONSOR
ROLE:	To sponsor the RAD project for management
QUALITIES:	A respected leader in the organization
NO. REQUIRED:	1
EXAMPLES:	Divisional manager
	Vice president
	Director of data processing
	Business area manager

Information Specialists

Information specialists are there to help the end users and to develop a design according to the end users' needs. Under the direction of the RAD facilitator, information specialists will need to create prototypes after discussing the requirements, so detailed knowledge of prototyping software is required.

They can also advise end users on new technology or hardware that can assist in the technical implementation. They need to understand the organization and the business area involved. Information specialists should be good listeners and empathize with end users. Experienced systems analysts who can use software have been excellent in this role. The box below summarizes this.

RAD ROLE PROFILE

TITLE:	INFORMATION SPECIALISTS
ROLE:	To develop the design according to the end users needs

QUALITIES:	Good technical skills
	Prototyping capability
	Ability to work with end users
	Empathy and patience
NO. REQUIRED:	Minimum 2, maximum 4
EXAMPLES:	Systems analysts
	Analyst programmers

The Scribe

The scribe has a particularly important role in the RAD team. He or she is responsible for documenting the RAD sessions. This is done in an interactive fashion, and the scribe must work closely with the RAD facilitator.

Many ideas and suggestions will be discussed. The scribe must learn to capture the important decisions made, who made them, and why. The scribe must compile and document what was discussed. Laptop computers become particularly useful in processing this information because they are portable.

During RAD sessions, it is important to encourage end users to call on the scribe to "make sure that point is documented." The scribe does not have to be an IT person but requires a logical approach to handling documentation. It is the responsibility of the scribe to distribute the documentation at the end of each RAD session. It is a difficult task and not to be underestimated. The box below summarizes this.

RAD ROLE PROFILE	
TITLE:	SCRIBE
ROLE:	To document the RAD sessions

QUALITIES:	Good logical skills
	Knowledge of word processing packages
	Good organizational skills
	Good administrative skills
NO. REQUIRED:	1
EXAMPLES:	Departmental secretary
	Systems analyst

Specialists

Depending on the type of RAD session, it is almost always a requirement that the team call on specialists' advice for the solution to some problem. It is not normally necessary for specialists to attend every RAD session because they may be needed for only a short while or part of a day. It is helpful if the RAD facilitator can describe in advance of the session what is required from the specialist. This ensures that maximum benefit is obtained and that the time is spent wisely. Examples of specialists include:

- Database designers, architects, administrators, or modelers
- Network specialists and designers
- System programmers, administrators, or specialists
- End-user specialists, experts, or business process designers

Specialized knowledge will often play an important role in a RAD environment, and the short-term help of specialists will provide valuable solutions.

Observers

When RAD is successfully introduced to an organization, word gets out quickly, and it generates interest from other projects and teams. The RAD facilitator will receive requests for observers who wish to see for themselves how RAD sessions work and decide whether it will work for them. Generally, the RAD facilitator and the team as a whole should encourage this. Care should be taken, however, that observers do not obstruct or hinder the progress of the RAD sessions. Often, observers join in the discussion or offer advice on issues because they quickly understand the group dynamics. The RAD facilitator should introduce all observers to the group at the beginning of each session.

▶ Conclusions

Clearly, RAD has many qualities and attractions that make it successful for many types of corporations. In the age of Internet speed and competitive edge, RAD gives many IT departments the success it badly needs.

However, there are many pitfalls and obstacles to successful adoption and implementation of its techniques. RAD is not easy at first but can be successful with experienced project managers who adopt and embrace the techniques described here. As project managers develop track records of successful RAD projects, significant improvements in productivity and speed will be seen. Some of these are:

- **Success**—Overall success can be attributed to an able, experienced RAD facilitator/project manager who can solve problems, meet deadlines, get results from people, and communicate.
- **Teamwork**—The complete team must pull together, with all members making a significant contribution to the effort and solution.
- **Tools**—Careful selection of tools is vital for success. All members of the RAD team who use the software must be experienced, capable, and willing to produce results quickly.
- **Communication**—With rapid development and its problems, it is vital that the RAD facilitator be a good communicator, dealing realistically with problems, and that he or she be forthright and direct. The person should be equally comfortable when communicating with presidents or programmers.
- **Scope**—As indicated earlier, the scope of the application must be agreed and fixed. There is no room for "scope creep" or the "WIBNI effect" (wouldn't it be nice if) from end users. Produc-

ing a working application in 30, 60, or 90 days takes discipline, understanding, and hard work.

- **People**—People make RAD successful.

▶ Suggested Readings

Gane, Chris. *Rapid System Development: Using Structured Techniques and Relational Technology.* Prentice Hall, 1989.

Martin, James. *Rapid Application Development.* McGraw Hill, 1991.

McConnell, Steve C. *Rapid Development: Taming Wild Software Schedules.* Microsoft Press, 1996.

Managing Risks

▶ Introduction

Risks are those unexpected events that cause problems—sometimes severe problems—which threaten the success of IT projects. Risk Management is where a project manager expresses his or her concerns about the probable effects of risks and the uncertain environment that they create. Because the future cannot be predicted with any degree of certainty, project managers have to consider a range of possible events that could take place. Risks could have a material effect (a significant consequence) on the enterprise and its goals. These negative effects are called *risks*, and the positive effects are called *opportunities*.

A manageable and repeatable process can be devised to manage risk on any size of project—large, medium, or small.

Several factors can influence the success of risk management:

- Senior management's expectations about risk—do they understand the value of risk management and, if not, how can they be persuaded?

161

- The corporate culture and attitudes toward accountability—is there a culture that can accept the need for accountability?

- The background, skills, and experience of the project teams— management of risks should be an important skill for *all* project teams.

Senior IT management, CIOs, and project managers must be responsible for ensuring that there are adequate policies and procedures for conducting risk management on both a long-range and day-to-day basis. This responsibility includes ensuring that there are clear lines of responsibility for managing risk, adequate systems for measuring risk, appropriately structured limits on risk taking, effective internal controls, and a comprehensive risk-reporting process. Many a career has been cut short because of failure to identify and manage risks.

▶ What Can Happen with No Risk Management

Barings Bank was one of the oldest merchant banks in London. Founded in 1765, it operated for over 230 years before its collapse in 1995. It survived wars, economic depressions, and turbulence but could not sustain the billions of dollars in losses caused by a single rogue trader. Nicholas Leeson, who was based in Singapore, traded (or rather gambled away) the entire financial assets of the bank. How did this happen? *The bank did not have sufficient risk management procedures in place to halt the decline.*

Once the symbol of sound investment banking, Barings was eventually sold for one pound sterling (approximately $1.65 U.S.). The collapse of Barings and the billions of dollars in losses suffered by other institutions, such as Sumitomo Corporation and BCCI Bank in London, catapulted the need for sound risk management into corporate consciousness. However, even before these spectacular losses, risk management had occupied the minds of those whose business it is to know—the regulators and the senior managers of the world's leading corporations. They knew that sound internal risk control is essential to the prudent operation of a corporation and to promoting stability of the global economy as a whole.

Information Technology Risk Management Objectives

The overall objectives for managing risk are straightforward and direct:

- To identify any risk—large or small—that might be a threat to the success of a project.
- To focus attention on minimizing these risks with appropriate corrective action.
- To provide a formal management and repeatable process approach for:
  - Identifying and assessing risks.
  - Determining effective risk reduction actions.
  - Monitoring and reporting progress in reducing risk.

Types of Risk in Project Management

Broadly, there are five main categories of risk types associated with project management.

1. External Risks

   External events are mainly outside the control of the project manager and, in most cases, the corporation. Examples include:

   - Marketplace developments—rapid developments can cause an abrupt change of direction
   - Government regulatory changes
   - Industry-specific procedures—new standards, issues
   - Mergers/acquisitions
   - Legal issues—disputes, lawsuits, and court orders
   - Change-driven factors—new products, services, changes in market
   - Corporate strategy and priority changes
   - Disasters such as fire, flood, earthquake, or other natural disaster

- Interference from outside electrical sources, causing disruption
- Loss of power, heating, or ventilation; air conditioning failure
- Sabotage, hacking, and security breaches
- Communications systems and security sensor failures
- Viruses and other malicious attacks on information systems
- Emergency destruction of communications

Most of these risks are very difficult to control at the project manager level but can be identified and, therefore, managed. This means that senior management must be involved in the risk management process and have input into risk control issues.

2. Cost Risks

Many of these types of risks are directly or indirectly under the project manager's control or within his or her area of influence. Examples of cost risks include those arising from:

- Cost overruns by project teams or subcontractors, vendors, and consultants
- Scope creep, expansion, and change that has not been managed
- Poor estimating or errors that result in unforeseen costs
- Overrun of budget and schedule

3. Schedule Risks

Schedule risks can cause project failure by missing or delaying a market opportunity for a product or service. Such risks are caused by:

- Inaccurate estimating, resulting in errors
- Increased effort to solve technical, operational, and external problems
- Resource shortfalls, including staffing delays, insufficient resources, and unrealistic expectations of assigned resources
- Unplanned resource assignment—loss of staff to other, higher-priority projects

4. Technology Risks

Technology risks can result from a wide variety of circumstances. The result is failure to meet systems' target functionality or performance expectations. Typical examples are:

- Problems with immature technology
- Use of the wrong tools
- Software that is untested or fails to work properly
- Requirement changes with no change management
- Failure to understand or account for product complexity
- Integration problems
- Software/hardware performance issues—poor response times, bugs, errors

5. Operational Risks

Operational risks are characterized by an inability to implement large-scale change effectively. Such risks can result in failure to realize the intended or expected benefits of the project. Typical causes are:

- Inadequate resolution of priorities or conflicts
- Failure to designate authority to key people
- Insufficient communication or lack of communication plan
- Size of transaction volumes—too great or too small
- Rollout and implementation risks—too much, too soon

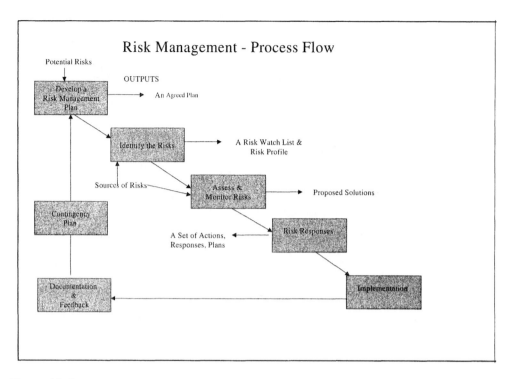

Figure 13–1   Process Flow for Project Risk Management

▶ The Risk Management Process

Figure 13–1 is an illustration of how project managers might manage risks in IT projects. This is only one example of the many processes that exist.

▶ Risk Management Plan

As Figure 13-1 shows, begin all project initiation with a plan. A risk management plan needs to be completed for all projects. It can be incorporated as a segment or part of an overall project plan. For smaller projects of less than 24 months' duration, the project manager should be responsible for compiling the risks. However, expect to assign a full-time resource to managing risk management for bigger or more complex projects. This plan must address all of the elements of the risk management process, including:

- Identifying the risks
- Determining the scope of risk management
- Establishing timelines, deliverables, milestones
- Assigning resources—who will be managing these risks?
- Developing a contingency plan

This plan requires a type of management as for any other project plan and must be kept accurate and up to date.

Identifying the Risks

The task of identifying potential risks is highly critical, and the project team must allocate sufficient time to accomplish it with quality and accuracy. This task must include JAD sessions or brainstorming to identify and prioritize risks that can possibly threaten the success of the project. Risks should be classified as having low, medium, or high probability of occurrence by questioning the likelihood of the risk event's occurrence. The next step is to specify the severity of impact to the project. Is an identified risk trivial or severe? Can it be eliminated from the assessment? Once all risks have been identified, they can be prioritized into a scale of occurrence or likelihood of impact.

Some risk methodologies use a numerical formula or weighting, which helps in quantifying the risk in this process. To use the numerical method, three areas are reviewed for evaluating risk and assigning scores:

1. Likelihood of occurrence—how likely is the risk?
2. Severity of impact—how severely will it impact the project?
3. Level of controllability—how controllable will it be?

Risk managers assign a value from 1 to 5 for each risk. A value of 1 means that it is unlikely to occur, and a value of 5 indicates near certainty. Table 13–1 contains the values and their descriptions.

Table 13–1 Risk Likelihood Scores

Assessment of Risk Likelihood	Value
Very unlikely to occur	1
Somewhat unlikely	2
Equal chance	3
Highly possible	4
Nearly certain	5

Next, analyze the severity of the risk's potential impact. How severe is the risk? Assign a value to the severity, based on the descriptions listed in Table 13–2.

Table 13–2 Risk Severity Scores

Assessment of Severity	Value
Minor impact on cost, schedule, performance, etc.	1
Moderate impact on cost, schedule, performance, etc.	2
Significant impact on project	3
Very significant impact on project	4
Catastrophic, disastrous impact, total project failure	5

Finally, determine the level of control over the risk. What can the project manager or organization do to control or mitigate the risk? Assign a value representing the level of control, based on the descriptions listed in Table 13–3.

Table 13–3 Level of Risk Control

Assessment of Controllability	Value
Avoidable through selected project mitigation actions	1
Highly controllable through project actions	2
Moderately controllable through project actions	3
Largely uncontrollable by the project	4

(continued)

Table 13–3 Level of Risk Control *(continued)*

Assessment of Controllability	Value
Uncontrollable and high risk of project failure	5

These techniques and tables are helpful in obtaining numerical values for risks. Individual methodologies will vary in assigning risk values; however, the techniques are basically the same. Generally, the score that each risk now receives is the product of the three values multiplied together. This provides a ranking of each risk and can be used to determine which risk is most critical to the project.

Risk Watch List

The deliverable from these efforts will be a document that contains a list of all the risks to monitor. The document is reviewed at regular project control meetings, perhaps even weekly, and updated with new developments or increases in risk. A sample risk list is shown in Table 13–4.

All of the data in this report can be obtained by using the techniques described above.

Assess and Monitor Risks

Risk management is not something that can be done once and forgotten. It is important to monitor and assess all risks continually, using the risk watch list. The objective in working with this document is to reduce or mitigate the identified risks. The risk management team will need to meet regularly—weekly, at a minimum. If the risks are severe, more frequent meetings are required, perhaps daily.

Project managers should be vigilant to risks. There is no room for complacency in risk management. A continuous process of documentation, feedback, and document revision is necessary to ensure the proper level of alertness. It is necessary to report on current risks, mitigation procedures, and risks that might reoccur.

Table 13–4 A Sample Risk List Document

Risk Number	Description of Risk	Risk Response	Severity of Impact (0–5)	Likelihood of Occurrence (0–5)	Significance Level (Impact + Likelihood)	Level of Control	Completion Date
1	Order entry system not delivered on time	Construct bridge to existing order entry system	4	5	9	5	Change request pending
2	Skilled personnel having early roll-off dates	Hire experienced personnel	2	4	6	3	Complete
3	User training for new billing system not complete by implementation	Use billing system development experts to conduct basic, jump-start training	3	3	6	2	In process

Contingency

For some risks, it will be necessary to draw up contingency plans that can be initiated and executed when a risk is threatening or a risk event occurs. Contingency plans are a lot like insurance: You may never need them, but without a contingency plan, the consequences of risk events could be devastating. Examples of these kinds of consequences are:

- Loss of vital records, files, and data
- Loss of communications systems
- Possible failure of computer security systems
- Inability to use mission-critical services or functions
- Extended periods of operating at less than normal efficiency
- Business disruption or outright failure
- A worst case—injury or death of employees

Also, like insurance policies, many organizations view contingency planning as unnecessary overhead. However, the expense of the entire contingency plan can be easily justified by reviewing the costs of a severe exposure to a business risk.

Good contingency plans must also come with detailed guidelines, checklists, worksheets, and project team support that describe clearly what to do and how to execute the contingency plan. Contingency plans often go hand in hand with disaster recovery procedures.

One final piece of advice: Test the contingency plan thoroughly, review it regularly, and revise is as necessary. An out-of-date contingency plan is useless. When revisions to the plan are made, be sure to inform anyone involved of the change, ensure that everyone has a current copy, and remove or destroy the previous versions to be sure that no one is working with old information.

▶ Enterprise Risk Profile

Once risk management is an established and effective management technique used by all projects and a broad based body of knowledge is built up within an enterprise, a risk profile can be constructed at the enterprise level. This profile states how the enterprise behaves in managing its risks. Projects using risk management feed data to the profile, and a model is built and analyzed. Trend analysis can be done to indicate which risks are the most problematic. If project failure rates are high, trends can be established, and corrective action can be taken. Questions such as which risk mitigation factors worked and which did not can be answered using an enterprise model approach. Analyzing failures is not a task that is done much in IT but, by doing so, many improvements can be made. We have done much with best practices— we should also devote time and analysis to worst practices.

A profile model of this type does take some time to develop. For example, 12 months of data are often needed before it can be representative and meaningful. However, with the prospect of risk trends at the IT enterprise level, the business case for developing a risk profile is compelling.

▶ Conclusions

There are some important conclusions we can draw about risk management and its effects on project management.

1. In the past, risk management has not been a discipline that has been embraced as much as it should have been within the IT industry. It was not important, and this short-term arrogance has sometimes cost us dearly. Consequently, we have learned the hard way about not managing risks and threats and about not having alternatives or a strategy to execute.

2. Senior IT management who will be managing risks at their own levels must drive risk management. If this is not forthcoming, project managers should recommend or propose a business case for implementing risk management.

3. Training is important. Risk managers, like project managers, are not born, they are created. Ensure that risk is on the corporate training schedule.

4. Risk management should be used for all projects—large, medium, or small. It is not a matter of scale or size. Risks can come in many different disguises; they do not discriminate about organization type, project size, or duration. Long, com-

plex projects are risky. A series of shorter projects is preferable. A trend is now in place to reduce consciously the size of projects that corporations undertake.

Corporations vary widely in their abilities to identify and manage risk at the IT level. In this fast-paced, fast cycle time of the new millennium, risks are going to exist more frequently, many times from unexpected sources. A management approach to containing then mitigating them and, perhaps, turning threats into opportunities is *necessary and mandatory.*

▶ Suggested Readings

Additional resources are available for the following topics:

Risk Management

Graham, John D. and Hartwell, Jennifer Kassalow, eds. *The Greening of Industry. A Risk Management Approach.* Harvard University Press, 1997.

Head, George L. and Horn, Stephen II. *Essentials of Risk Management, Volumes I & II.* Insurance Institute, 1991, 8 vols., 240 pp.

Schwartz, Robert J. and Smith, Clifford W. *Advanced Strategies in Financial Risk Management.* Prentice Hall, 1993.

Uyemura, Dennis G. and Van Deventer, Donald R. *Financial Risk Management in Banking.* Bankers Publishing Company, c. 1993. Note: Interesting reading on how banks manage their risk.

Information Technology Project Management Risk

Beenhakker, Henri L. *Risk Management in Project and Implementation.* Quorum Books, 1997, 274 pp.

Chapman, Chris and Ward, Stephen. *Project Risk Management: Processes, Techniques and Insights.* John Wiley & Sons, 1997. Author recommended.

Covello, Vincent T., Menkes, Joshu,a and Mumpower, Jeryl. *Risk Evaluation and Management. Contemporary Issues in Risk Analysis, Volume 1*. Plenum Press, 1986, 544 pp.

DeWeaver, Mary Feeherry and Gillespie, Lori Ciprian. *Real-World Project Management: New Approaches for Adapting to Change and Uncertainty*. Quality Resources, 1997.

Kliem, Ralph L. and Ludin, Irwin S. *Reducing Project Risk*. Gower Publishing, 1997, revised edition, 228 pp.

Obradovitch, M.M. and Stephanou, S.E. *Project Management: Risks & Productivity*. David Spencer, 1990. Royal 8 vols., 438 pp.

Chapter

14

Managing Problems

▶ Introduction

In the IT industry, we are constantly faced with problems and the need to solve them. The industry, by its nature and the inherent level of complexity, forces us daily to face a barrage of different types of problems from simple to complex and some that even appear to be unsolvable.

Consider for a moment the very wide range of problems we face:

- Technical—hardware, software, infrastructure
- Network—making networks work
- Management—project-related, end users
- Resource—getting the right staff
- Cultural—working with others who are different
- Quality—ensuring that projects work well
- Managing change—the rapid pace of change
- Legal—copyright, patent, law suits
- Bureaucratic—getting agreement
- Environmental—making the right choices
- Financial problems—budgets, cost control

175

- Internet—use, access, and volume of data
- Industry-specific—generally, keeping up with the rate of change
- Federal/state—new laws, regulations, and changes
- Personal—family, stress, health, and finances

Although this list is only a sample, it does illustrate the wide scope and variety of problems we face. Not all of them are unique to IT project management, but many are. The key issue then is, *how do we go about solving problems?*

In the past, we have tackled problems and worked on them until we are satisfied that they are solved. Basically, we use our own individual experiences and expertise to solve problems. Project managers are faced with many more problems than are other managers. Maybe we should change their titles to problem managers, rather than project managers. Good project managers are skilled at solving problems quickly and effectively. How do they achieve this skill?

Several studies have been conducted by "think tanks" and universities to understand how problems occur, what the symptoms are, and what the best and appropriate techniques are for solving them. Many techniques are now available, but one dominant theme is apparent in these studies: *Problem solving can really be effective by using a repeatable process—a methodology or organized approach to problem solving.*

Good managers systematically ask questions, interview and document, understand the problem dimensions, prioritize, then formulate solutions, implement, and monitor.

▶ Who Uses Problem Solving?

The simple answer is: anyone who has a problem. Problem-solving techniques can be used on an individual basis or by complete project teams. If the problem is large, it is advisable for more than one person to work on it. The project management rule of "divide and conquer" applies here. It is the repeatable process that is important—not the number of people using it.

Using problem-solving techniques requires appropriate training. It is not sufficient merely to read books or manuals and attempt to solve

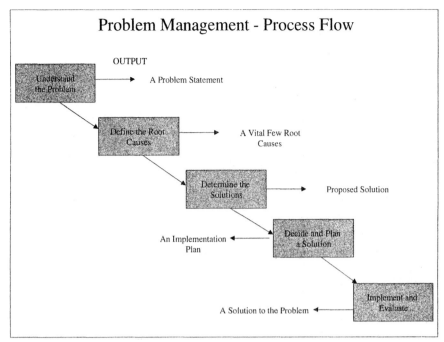

Figure 14–1   The Problem Management Process

problems. Trainers need to observe the team to ensure that the process is being followed and that quality results are being generated.

▶ The Problem Solving Model

We shall now discuss a general model for problem solving. This approach is effective and can be applied to the IT industry. It is based on the Kepner-Tregoe model.

There are five steps in this model, illustrated in Figure 14–1.

1. Understand the problem

    -   Define the problem
    -   Describe its dimensions
    -   Collect and analyze data
    -   Write a problem statement

2. Define the root causes

- Analyze the problem's dimensions
- List the suspected causes
- Prioritize to a few root causes

3. Determine the solutions

- Seek potential solutions
- Evaluate to a few solutions
- Determine the best solution

4. Decide and plan

- Create implementation plan
- Get management agreement on plan
- Staff, resource if needed

5. Implement and evaluate

- Implement the solution
- Monitor the solution
- Collect performance data
- Fine-tune the solution
- Celebrate success

Understand the Problem

Before you can solve a problem, it is essential to understand it. This involves investigation work to determine the dimensions and extent of the problem. Broadly, we define a problem as a deviation from an expected level of performance whose cause is unknown.

To understand the problem at hand, the team should be asking pertinent questions, such as:

- When does the problem occur?
- Who is impacted?

- What are the characteristics/complaints/symptoms?
- How often does it happen?
- What is the magnitude?
- Is there any evidence, statistics, or data that can be collected?

These questions are essential for determining the overall problem size and the gaps in the process. The output from this step will be a *problem statement,* which is a written document that explains the problem. This document can then be sent to the business units or end users affected by the problem to confirm that it is accurate and reflects the true nature and understanding of the problem under investigation. It is important to avoid proposing any solutions or the root causes at this stage. This will be done later.

The basis for an eventual solution will be developed from factual data that will be collected. This data needs to be collected over a period of time to verify the problem. The project team might need to present the data in a graphical format that is much better for management to understand, using pie charts, histograms, or Pareto Diagrams and charts.

When this step is completed and agreement is reached that a strongly worded and comprehensive problem statement exists, a good foundation exists on which to build a solution. The project team should not underestimate the amount of time this stage takes. Problem definition cannot be completed rapidly and requires good investigative techniques.

Define the Root Causes

After a problem statement is agreed upon, it will now be necessary to probe deeper and to ask the essential question, *Why does this happen?* There may be multiple causes to a problem, but each time, the question should be asked to reveal a more deeply rooted cause.

We can define the root cause as the most basic factor(s) that, if eliminated or removed, would prevent the problem from happening or reoccurring. The project team can use any number of known techniques, such as brainstorming, JAD sessions, and process review, to list the root causes. There may also be suspected causes, which need to be further investigated and clarified to determine the few actual root causes.

Determine the Solutions

The next step is to take the few root causes identified in the previous step and generate potential solutions. This should be a course of action designed to eliminate the problem. The project team must decide how it will recognize when the appropriate solutions are uncovered. The team needs to compile a set of decision objectives. This is a method of determining what success in problem management will be. Once the objectives are agreed upon, the team will then be able to list potential solutions.

The team needs to be able to generate solutions to the problem. This might be new software/hardware, but it might mean changes at the enterprise level, such as:

- Changes in process flows/workflows
- Staffing changes
- New procedures or policies
- New forms of automation
- Structural organization changes
- Capturing new data
- New training
- Quality audits
- Outside assistance/consulting
- Implementation of service-level agreements (SLAs)

The ultimate solution may be a combination of these factors and should be in the best interests of the enterprise.

Decide and Plan

Like all good projects, after determining the best solution, an implementation plan needs to be constructed. It is then presented to management. Careful attention is needed to make sure that the business case for solving the problem is sound and realistic. A key word here is that the solution is "defensible."` That is, it will stand up to the most corrosive criticisms. If the project team has done all of the steps outlined here, there should be no problems in defending the proposed solution.

Implement and Evaluate

The final steps include implementing and monitoring the solution. It is important to determine that the problem is finally going away and that the solution is, indeed, working. Achieving this level of satisfaction requires validation of performance data and, invariably, fine-tuning and making adjustments to the solution.

Once this is achieved, the project team should be celebrating success. Job well done! Time to start on the next problem.

A Matrix Guide

Table 14–1 is a matrix that lists the forms and worksheets that are used in each of the five steps in the model. It indicates where the form is created and used.

Table 14-1 Matrix of Forms and Documents Used in Problem Management

Project Forms/ Worksheets	1. Understand the Problem	2. Define the Root Causes	3. Determine the Solutions	4. Decide and Plan	5. Implement and Evaluate
Problem-Solving Project Plan	Created here	Used here	Used here	Used here	Used here
Problem Statement	Created here	Used here	Used here	-	-
Problem Dimension Statement	Created here	Used here	Used here	-	-
Suspected Causes List	-	Created here	Used here	-	-
Vital Few Root Causes List	-	Created here	Used here	-	-
Solutions List	-	-	Created here	Used here	-
Solution Business Case	-	-	Created here	Used here	-
Implementation Plan	-	-	-	Created here	Used Here

A LARGE MIDWESTERN BANK

Source: Author's personal experience

A large Midwestern Bank based in Chicago with assets over $235 billion and 1,800 branches in 15 states had experienced very rapid growth through mergers and acquisitions. With over 1,800 mainframe computer applications running in multiple data centers around the country, it began to experience disrupted service to customers, unreliable production systems, and many other symptoms of growth. Files were late, JCL errors occurred, ATM networks went down, and new systems failed, due to insufficient testing.

The bank's senior management became concerned and put together a problem management team to define procedures to reduce the number of errors. The team used the process described here for about three months. It analyzed the errors, collected data on the problems, documented a problem statement, and determined the root causes.

The team came up with multiple recommendations and solutions:

- Implement a daily Service Excellence Program to improve performance and quality.

- Track and define all errors daily, using an enterprise-wide database.

- Define a root cause for all serious errors (over 1,000 customers affected or more than $1 million in lost revenue was considered to be a serious error).

- Define trends, causes, and action items to improve quality and reliability.

- Implement SLAs defining the terms of operations, outputs, support, and so on for all major systems.

- Devise a bonus and incentive plan by application to reduce programmers' errors.

- Construct a Performance Board of senior managers to review monthly statistics trends on overall performance.

The bank's senior management agreed and supported all of the recommendations. After one year of operation, the number of production problems fell by over 40%. This was translated into a savings of over $400 million.

▶ Other Problem Management Techniques

There are other techniques that complement or supplement this problem management approach and can be useful in problem solving.

- Brainstorming—generating options and evaluating new approaches
- Analyzing the strengths, weaknesses, opportunities, and threats (SWOT)
- Lateral thinking—thinking up new or unusual solutions to problems
- Force field analysis—deciding on factors for or against change
- JAD—an integrated team approach to analysis or design
- Critical path analysis—planning and implementing complex projects
- Iterative management—revisiting a problem until solved
- Incremental management—solving problems in small portions
- Decomposition—breaking down a problem to simpler layers

Some of these techniques are described further in Chapter 15.

▶ Conclusions

The technique described here is only one of many problem management techniques. However, it illustrates the need for a formalized process—a repeatable process to achieve a solution. Depending on the size, nature, and origin of the problem, a shortened or accelerated process could be used for faster results.

Most corporations now realize the value of having problem management techniques, and the most mature organizations have gained benefits and are using problem management techniques similar to those described here. The important theme throughout this chapter has been to select and use a repeatable problem process.

▶ Suggested Readings

Costa, Victoria Brookhar, "School Science as a Rite of Passage; A New Frame for Familiar Problems." *J of R in Science Teaching*. 1993; 30(7):649–668.

Dall'Alba, Gloria et al. "Textbook Treatment of Problem Understanding." *J Res Sci Teaching*. 1993:30(7):621–635.

Halloun, Ibrahim A., and Hestenes, David. "Common Sense Concepts about Problems." *Am J Phys*. 1987;53(1056).

Heller, T. L., and Reif, F. "Prescribing Effective Human Problem-Solving Processes: Problem Solving in Cognition and Instruction." *Cogn Instruction*. 1984;1(2):177.

Howard Margolis. *Patterns, Thinking, and Cognition*. Chicago: University of Chicago Press, 1987.

Newell, Allen. *Unified Theories of Cognition*. Harvard University Press, 1990.

Newell, Allen, and Simon, Herbert A. *Human Problem Solving*. Prentice Hall, 1972.

Reif, Frederick. "Millikan Lecture 1994: Understanding and Teaching Important Scientific Thought Processes." *Am J Phys*. 1995;63(1):17–32.

Staver, J. R. "The Effects of Problem Format, Number of Independent Variables, and Their Interaction on Student Performance on a Control of Variable Reasoning Problem." *J Res Sci Teaching*. 1986;23(6):533–542.

Sternberg, Robert. *Beyond IQ*. Cambridge University Press, 1984.

Polya, Gyargy. *How to Solve It*. Princeton University Press, 1945. Historical interest.

Whimbey, Arthur, "Think Aloud Pair Solving—APS; The Key to Higher Order Thinking in Precise Processing." *Educ Leadership.* 1987;42(1):66–70.

Other Techniques

▶ Introduction

In this chapter, we will review some of the many other techniques used in managing projects. It is a quick look at the style, approaches, and, in some cases, the methodology used.

▶ Software Quality Assurance

The purpose of Software Quality Assurance (SQA) is to provide management with clarity into the process being used by the software project and of the products being built.

SQA involves reviewing and auditing the software products, processes, procedures, tasks, and milestones to verify that they comply with the applicable standards and providing the project managers and other senior management with the results of these reviews and audits.

The SQA group works with the software project during its early stages to establish plans, standards, and procedures that will add value to the software project and satisfy the project constraints and the organiza-

187

tion's policies. By participating in establishing these plans, standards, and procedures, the software quality assurance group helps to ensure that they fit the project's needs and verifies that they will be usable for performing reviews and audits throughout the software lifecycle. The SQA group reviews project tasks and audits software work products throughout the SDLC lifecycle and provides management with visibility as to whether the software project is adhering to its established objectives and standards.

This key process area covers the practices for the group performing the software quality assurance function. The practices identifying the specific tasks and work products that the SQA reviews and/or audits are generally contained in the Verifying Implementation common feature of the other key process areas.

The goals of SQA are:

1. All SQA tasks are planned.
2. Adherence of software products and tasks to the applicable standards, procedures, and requirements is verified objectively.
3. Affected groups and individuals are informed of SQA tasks and results.
4. Noncompliance issues that cannot be resolved within the software project are addressed by senior management.

The high-level tasks performed for SQA are:

1. An SQA plan is prepared for the software project according to a documented procedure.
2. The SQA group's activities are performed in accordance with the SQA plan.
3. The SQA group participates in the preparation and review of the project's software development plan, standards, and procedures.
4. The SQA group reviews the software engineering activities to verify compliance.
5. The SQA group audits designated application development projects' work products to verify compliance.
6. The SQA group periodically reports the results of its activities to the software engineering group.

7. Deviations identified in the software activities and software work products are documented and handled according to a documented procedure.

8. The SQA group conducts periodic reviews of its activities and findings with the customer's SQA personnel, as appropriate.

▶ Configuration Management

The purpose of configuration management (CM) is to establish and maintain the integrity of the products of the software project throughout the software lifecycle.

CM involves identifying the configuration of the software (i.e., selected software work products and their descriptions) at given points in time, systematically controlling changes to the configuration and maintaining the integrity and traceability of the configuration throughout the software lifecycle. This traceability is often tracked using a matrix. The work products placed under configuration management include the software products that are delivered to the customer/client (e.g., the software requirements document and the source code) and the items that are identified with or required to create these software products (e.g., the compiler).

A baseline is established containing the software products as they are developed. Changes to baselines and the release of software products built from the software baseline library are systematically controlled via the change control and configuration auditing functions of software CM.

This process covers the practices for performing the CM function. The practices for identifying specific configuration items/units are contained in the key process areas that describe the development and maintenance of each configuration item/unit. It is important to manage the entire configuration—hence its name.

The goals of CM are:

1. Configuration management activities are planned and a plan exists.

2. Selected software work products are identified, controlled, and available.

3. Changes to identified software work products are controlled.

4. Affected groups and individuals are informed of the status and content of software baselines.

▶ Requirements Management

Requirements management is a technique for establishing a common understanding between the client, end user or management, and the software project of the customer's requirements that will be addressed by the software project deliverables.

Requirements management involves establishing and maintaining an agreement with the customer on the requirements for the software project. This agreement is referred to as the *system requirements allocated to the software*. The "customer" may be interpreted as the system engineering group, the marketing group, another internal organization, or an external customer. The agreement covers both the technical and nontechnical issues (e.g., resources, milestones, and requirements). The agreement forms the basis for estimating, planning, performing, and tracking the software project's activities throughout the entire SDLC cycle.

The allocation of the system requirements to software, hardware, and other resources may be performed by a group external to the project team (e.g., the system engineering group), and the project team may have no direct control of this allocation. Within the constraints of the project, the project team takes appropriate steps to ensure that the system requirements allocated to software, which they are responsible for addressing, are documented and controlled.

To achieve this control, the project team reviews the initial and revised system requirements allocated to software to resolve issues before they are incorporated into the software project. Whenever the system requirements allocated to software are changed, the affected software plans, work products, and activities are adjusted to remain consistent with the updated requirements.

The goals of requirements management are:

1. Project-specific requirements allocated to software are controlled to establish a baseline for software engineering and management use.

2. All software plans, products, and activities are kept consistent with the system requirements allocated to software.

The high-level tasks performed for requirements management are:

1. The project team reviews the allocated requirements before they are incorporated into the software project.

2. The project team uses the allocated requirements as the basis for software plans, work products, and tasks.

3. Changes to the allocated requirements are reviewed and incorporated into the software project.

4. For very large projects, a requirements manager and a requirements team may be needed as a dedicated resource.

▶ SWOT Analysis

SWOT Analysis is an effective method of identifying your strengths and weaknesses and examining the opportunities and threats that you face. Often, carrying out an analysis using the SWOT framework will be enough to reveal useful changes that can be made. In a sense, it can also be considered to be a form of risk management. All members of the project team should participate, and each member should be given time to express his or her views.

To carry out a SWOT analysis, project teams need to answer to the following questions:

1. Strengths

- What are our advantages?
- What do we do well?

    Consider these questions from your own point of view and from the point of view of the people you deal with. Be realistic, not modest. If you are having any difficulty with this, try writing down a list of your characteristics. It is hoped that some of these will be strengths!

2. Weaknesses:

- What could be improved?
- What is done badly?
- What should be avoided?

Again, this should be considered from an internal and external basis. Do other people perceive weaknesses that you don't see? Do your competitors do any better? It is best to be realistic now and face any unpleasant truths as soon as possible. Be frank and open about the weaknesses.

3. Opportunities

- Where are the good tasks?
- What are the interesting trends?

Useful opportunities can come from such things as:

- Changes in technology and markets on both broad and narrow scales
- Changes in government policy related to your industry
- Changes in social patterns, population profiles, lifestyle, etc.
- Local events, national events, international events

4. Threats

- What obstacles do we face?
- What is our competition doing?
- Are the required specifications for your job, products, or services changing?
- Is changing technology threatening our position?
- Do we have management support?
- Do we have the right amount of resources?
- Is there scope creep? WIBNI (wouldn't it be nice if?).
- Are we using the right tools, software, and platforms?

Project teams and their managers need to carry out this analysis periodically. The results will often be illuminating, both in terms of pointing out what needs to be done and in putting problems into perspective.

▶ Release Management

The release manager is the controller of an application or system release who monitors the development and testing process, constantly evaluating project progress and alerting upper management to risks and issues. A release can also contain changes to the production support environment or architecture for requested changes. A release can be made up of many project sizes, complexities, and values. The manager uses information from the prior processes of change control initial scope definition/estimation and approval to assemble the list of prioritized change controls to be included in the release. Individual project managers and teams are selected, who then manage and develop the individual projects. The release manager oversees all of the documentation from a release charter and project charters through the release closure document. Once the release is installed, a core development team from the release moves into a production support role.

The goals of release management are:

1. To manage and implement software release successfully.
2. To manage and mitigate risks associated with the release.
3. To release software projects in an orderly manner.

The high-level tasks performed for release management are:

1. Negotiates and agrees on the content of the release with end users and management; publishes the release charter.
2. Selects and staffs project teams to accomplish the release.
3. Assesses the progress of releases; assesses test results and quality; compiles metrics.
4. Manages the release implementation and migration to production.
5. Evaluates the release after implementation and documents lessons learned.

▶ Software Subcontract Management

The purpose of software subcontract management is to select qualified software subcontractors and to manage them effectively. Software subcontract management involves selecting a software subcontractor, establishing commitments with the subcontractor, and tracking and reviewing the subcontractor's performance and results. These practices cover the management of a software (only) subcontract, as well as the management of the software component of a subcontract that includes software, hardware, and possibly other system components.

The subcontractor is selected based on its ability to perform the work. Many factors contribute to the decision to subcontract a portion of the prime contractor's work. Subcontractors may be selected based on strategic business alliances, as well as technical considerations. The practices of this key process area address the traditional acquisition process associated with subcontracting a defined portion of the work to another organization.

When subcontracting, a documented agreement covering the technical and nontechnical (e.g., delivery dates) requirements is established and is used as the basis for managing the subcontract. The work to be done by the subcontractor and the plans for the work are documented. The standards that are to be followed by the subcontractor are compatible with the prime contractor's standards.

The subcontractor performs tracking and oversight tasks for the subcontracted work. The prime contractor ensures that these planning, tracking, and oversight tasks are performed appropriately and that the software products delivered by the subcontractor satisfy their acceptance criteria that have been previously defined and agreed upon. The prime contractor works with the subcontractor to manage their product and process interfaces.

The goals of subcontract management are:

1. The prime contractor selects and manages one or more qualified subcontractors.

2. The prime contractor and the subcontractor agree to their commitments to each other by a mutual contract.

3. The prime contractor and the subcontractor maintain ongoing communications and regular status meetings.

4. The prime contractor tracks the subcontractor's actual results and performance against its commitments and contractual obligations.

The high-level tasks performed for subcontract management are:

1. The subcontractor is selected, based on an evaluation of the subcontract bidder's ability to perform the work, according to a documented and agreed-upon procedure, references, and other professional checks.
2. The work to be subcontracted is defined and planned according to a documented and agreed-upon procedure, a statement of work, and a project plan.
3. The contractual agreement between the prime contractor and the subcontractor is used as the basis for managing the subcontract.
4. A documented subcontractor's project plan is regularly reviewed and approved by the prime contractor.
5. A documented and approved subcontractor's project plan is used for tracking the software tasks and communicating status.
6. Changes to the subcontractor's statement of work, subcontract terms and conditions, and other commitments are resolved according to an agreed-upon documented procedure, including arbitration, if needed.
7. The prime contractor's management conducts periodic status/coordination audits or reviews with the subcontractor's management.
8. Periodic technical reviews and interchanges are held with the software subcontractor.
9. Formal reviews to address the subcontractor's project-specific accomplishments and results are conducted at selected milestones, according to a documented and agreed-upon procedure.
10. The prime contractor's SQA group monitors the subcontractor's SQA tasks, according to a documented and agreed-upon procedure.
11. The prime contractor's software configuration management group monitors the subcontractor's tasks for software configuration management, according to a documented and agreed-upon procedure.

12. The prime contractor conducts acceptance testing as part of the delivery of the subcontractor's software products, according to a documented and agreed-upon procedure.

13. The software subcontractor's performance is evaluated on a periodic basis, and the evaluation is reviewed with the subcontractor.

▶ Quality Reviews

The purpose of quality reviews is to remove defects from the software work products early and efficiently. An important effect is the development of a better understanding of the software work products and of defects that might be prevented. This avoids problems later on in the project lifecycle.

Quality reviews involve a methodical examination of software work products by the producers' peers to identify defects and areas where changes are needed. The specific products that will undergo a quality review are identified in the project's defined software process and scheduled as part of the software project planning tasks.

This key process area covers the practices for performing quality reviews. The practices identifying the specific software work products that undergo quality review are contained in the key process areas that describe the development and maintenance of each software work product. All projects should undergo quality reviews to reduce errors and improve the processes.

The goals of quality reviews are:

1. Review tasks are planned and scheduled at appropriate intervals in the project lifecycle.
2. Defects are identified and removed.
3. The process improvement is a continuous function.

The top-level tasks performed for quality reviews are:

1. Reviews are planned and scheduled; the plans are documented.
2. Reviews are performed by skilled staff, according to a documented procedure.

3. Data on the conduct and results of the reviews are reported.

4. Metrics are accumulated as empirical evidence and a foundation for future planning.

▶ Crisis Management

A crisis management team is comprised mainly of senior management. It manages the strategic response to the crisis, releases funds quickly, and ensures that the enterprise's values and ethics are applied. It controls the messages sent to stakeholders, media, employees, and those identified as being affected by the situation. The CEO should lead the team or a senior executive with enough clout and respect to gets things done. Crisis management is an extreme response to a project or business risk event, and the policies and procedures for crisis management should be developed and documented as part of the project contingency plan.

The team will be required to act rapidly when circumstances permit. It is responsible for actually tackling a crisis. Team members have the technical and business backgrounds to handle the specific consequences of the incident. Another important aspect of crisis management is communication. Communication is vital in a crisis. This team concentrates on communicating with the media, police, military, public, employees, and shareholders to dispense the news—both good and bad—and information concerning what is being done to rectify the situation.

The goals of crisis management are:

1. To respond rapidly to a crisis that is a threat to the organization.

2. To assemble a team to respond, act, and eliminate or control the crisis.

3. To communicate with all affected parties.

The top-level tasks performed for crisis management are:

1. Develop a crisis management plan. (See Appendix D for an example)

2. Understand the crisis triggers and respond to them at the crisis time.

3. Perform the tasks of the plan.

4. Communicate with the media, shareholders, general public, and any other affected parties.

Project managers can make very effective members of any Crisis Management team and have the training and experience to deal with a wide spectrum of challenges. Good managers can make decisions and act quickly to contain the crisis. For crises affecting IT operations, such as fire, flood, tornado, and earthquake, business continuity plans must be available to be implemented swiftly. For other enterprise-type crises, such as wrong data, recalls, or other types of data-related crises, a specific planning approach may be needed.

▶ Suggested Readings

Additional resources are available for the following topics:

Software Quality Assurance

Ginac, Frank P. *Customer-Oriented Software Quality Assurance*. Prentice Hall, 1997.

Perry, William E. *Quality Assurance for Information Systems: Methods, Tools, and Techniques*. John Wiley & Sons, 1991.

Schulmeyer, G. Gordon. *The Handbook of Software Quality Assurance*. Prentice Hall, 1998.

Configuration Management

Berlack, H. Ronald. *Software Configuration Management*. John Wiley & Sons, 1991.

Leon, Alexis. *A Guide to Software Configuration Management*. Artech House, 2000.

Lyons, David Douglas. *Practical CM: Best Configuration Management Practices for the 21st Century*. Raven Press, 1999.

Requirements Management

Mumford, Enid. *Effective Systems Design and Requirements Analysis: The Ethics Method*. MacMillan Publishing USA, 1995.

Wiley, Bill. *Essential System Requirements: A Practical Guide to Event-Driven Methods (Addison-Wesley Information Technology Series)*. Addison-Wesley Publishing Co., 1999.

SWOT Analysis

Johnson, Nick and Cooper, Simon. *SWOT—A Level Law*. William Gaunt & Sons, 1995.

Subcontract Management

Wangemann, Mary Ann P. *2000 Subcontract Management Manual*. Harcourt Brace & Company, 1999.

Quality Reviews

Kan, Stephen H. *Metrics and Models in Software Quality Engineering*. Addison-Wesley Publishing Co., 1995.

Crisis Management

Henry, Rene A. *You'd Better Have a Hose if You Want to Put Out the Fire: The Complete Guide to Crisis and Risk Communications*. MIT Press, 1992.

Lerbinger, Otto. *The Crisis Manager: Facing Risk and Responsibility*. Lawrence Erlbaum, 1996.

Regester, Michael and Larkin, Judy. *Risk Issues and Crisis Management: A Casebook of Best Practice*. Kogan Page, 1998.

Part 5

Special Topics in Project Management

Knowledge Management

*I do not think much of a man who is not wiser today than he was
yesterday.*
  Abraham Lincoln

▶ Introduction

Knowledge management (KM) is a relatively new set of technologies
that displays all the signs of a technology that will set a mega-trend for
those corporations that embrace it. At the present time, KM is little
understood but much talked about; there are many definitions, and
there is a considerable amount of media hype around the subject. KM
has been practiced intensively, successfully, and very profitably by large
consulting firms such as Andersen Consulting and others, together
with the larger Fortune 500 companies. Scientific and technical indus-
tries (e.g., pharmaceuticals) and large computer vendors (e.g., IBM) are
beginning to follow suit as the market for sales expands. KM is a key
component and an enabler of the "Knowledge Economy" that has
gained much media interest and has been referred to by politicians,
gurus, technology forecasters, and others over the past few years. It is
the subject of a burgeoning worldwide consulting business that the
Gartner Group estimates will grow to $4.5 billion in 2000 as consult-
ing companies transfer their expertise to clients.

203

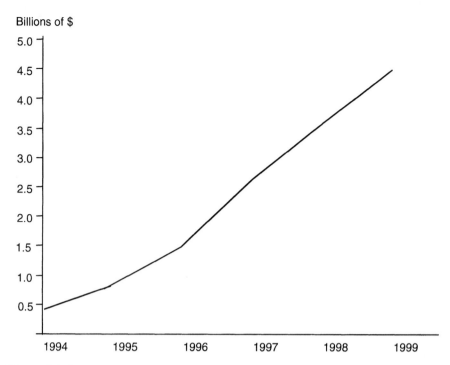

Billions of $

Figure 16–1   Sales of KM Software (1994–1999) (*Source: Dataquest*)

These figures represent by far a very conservative estimate and are almost certain to be revised upward substantially as research organizations garner more accurate statistics. Figure 16–1 illustrates the astounding growth of KM software sales.

KM is championed by numerous but, at present, mainly small technology vendors having products that claim to provide a wide range of benefits, both quantitative and qualitative. As the market grows and expands, this market will attract larger vendors, such as IBM and others, who will roll out products and services. This is beginning to happen at the writing of this book. Like previous efforts at management and technology-enabled transformation, such as total quality management (TQM) and business process reengineering (BPR), corporations that do not fully understand the real depth of cultural commitment and change required for success overestimate KM as a path to competitive advantage and higher profits. KM differs from BPR, TQM, and other trends in that it depends on exploiting technology infrastructure by the use of products such as a knowledge warehouse (KW)—a corporate repository of all knowledge, using intranets, middleware, software agents, and other products and utilities.

KM is also an emerging set of processes, organizational structures, applications, and technologies that aims to leverage the abilities of the individual employees, project teams, and business units to *act* quickly and effectively. KM achieves this end by providing ready access to the corporation's entire store of knowledge in a repository or KW, including much of what is known but not documented. KM requires an integrated approach to identifying, managing, and—most importantly—*sharing* the enterprise's information assets, including software, databases, documents, policies, and procedures (i.e., "explicit" knowledge), as well as undocumented expertise resident in individual workers (i.e., "tacit" knowledge).

KM differs from traditional software or information engineering approaches to *data sharing* in many ways, including an emphasis on *individual behavior* as opposed to *data standardization* as the primary means for achieving information sharing and leverage. This emphasis has important implications for the technologies used to support KM. The technologies, including groupware and information retrieval (IR), are collaborative; they complement (and are complemented by) earlier approaches to data sharing, including data warehousing and data mining. Whereas the latter approaches focus on providing access to highly structured (usually transaction-derived) data, KM provides access to large-grained, relatively *unstructured information* and the people who create it.

▶ Why Is KM Necessary?

Any successful enterprise has always managed its knowledge or intellectual capital at some level. Why is large-scale management of enterprise knowledge suddenly so important? The globalization of business, faster cycle times, and rapid responses necessary to the ever-changing marketplace are some of the reasons, as mentioned many times in this book. Geographic distribution of personnel results in the distribution of the enterprise's knowledge; without active management of that knowledge, there is no way to ensure that business practices will be consistent, effective, and representative at every point of "best practices" for the enterprise. The early adopters of large-scale KM intentionally have been global consulting organizations, such as Andersen Consulting. The market forces and strategies of these companies have helped to enable rapid worldwide implementation of their innovations. For such companies, KM is the price of leadership, and the corporations most likely to invest heavily in KM are those seeking *competitive advantage,* in particular, those for which competitive advantage is based on rapid delivery of high-quality, high-value products and services.

KM issues include developing, implementing, and maintaining the appropriate technical and organizational infrastructures to enable knowledge sharing and selecting specific contributing technologies and vendors. The decision to manage knowledge capital—to pursue maximum leverage for everything that the enterprise knows—is the result of a particular culture that sees organizational and personal power in certain ways. The never-ending quest of KM is *expensive, complex, and highly political*; yet, for many corporations, especially those that have invested heavily in highly skilled human resources, it is the next prerequisite business survival weapon. Corporate memory, intellectual capital, and KM all refer to the same idea: *leveraging and linking knowledge (documented and undocumented) within the enterprise.* Corporations are positioning KM as a discipline. To succeed, KM must be oriented to practical application of knowledge, e.g., in project management. It must show value and potential for profits and fast cycle times.

▶ Sources of Knowledge Capital

There are many potential sources for knowledge capital, internal and external to the enterprise. Anything that touches the enterprise is a potential source of information that leads the enterprise to adjust or replace its existing knowledge models. Knowledge capital enables an enterprise to make its models explicit, which makes those models subject to examination, improvement, and, if necessary, replacement.

A potential danger of knowledge capital is the pursuit and documentation of all knowledge known or knowable (similar to the over-modeling syndrome that characterized many Information Engineering efforts in the 1980s). An orientation toward application of practical knowledge and a culture of support for individual responsibility and excellence are key to success. Knowledge management is about leveraging information. Information is power, so long as it can be found and reused.

Knowledge sources are many and varied, including, but not limited to:

- All of the corporation's products and services
- All of the processes, designs, templates, and plans used to create products and services
- All types of software—customized and packages purchased on every mainframe and every PC
- Corporate data in databases, electronic documents, flat files, repositories, warehouses and marts, architectures, and PC files created by employees
- Information on vendors, suppliers, competitors
- Alliances and strategic relationships and their created data
- Customers and clients
- The Internet, newsgroups
- Research documents, reports, files, patents, trade secrets
- All of the corporation's technology and architectures
- All forms of digital, image, and nondigital data

CASE STUDIES

Corporate case studies abound and have produced spectacular results. Below are two of the many examples where KM has provided an exceptional return for the investment:

1. Texas Instruments avoided spending $500 million to build a new wafer fabrication plant by implementing KM practices. By sharing best knowledge over an intranet and a Lotus Notes database, TI's technicians boosted manufacturing capacity by an amount equal to the yield from a new plant.

2. A major oil company, Chevron, had two "best-practice" teams that saved the company over $170 million by sharing knowledge that had been scattered around the country. One team saved $150 million by sharing ways to reduce the use of electric power and fuel. Another saved Chevron $20 million by comparing data on gas compressors.

Source: Author's research

▶ The Potential for Project Management— KM for PM

Having read the foregoing, it does not take a genius to see the potential and value for project managers. The challenge that project managers face is transferring the know-how from inside people's heads into a shareable corporate form and continuously converting raw data into explicit knowledge.

Here we can list a few examples of how KM will benefit project management:

> *Project Management Repository*—can be implemented across the corporation providing all services and products related to project management. It should be made accessible to all teams and project managers, and should contain the items listed below. Where formats are a problem, for example, with different word processors, automatic converters, and filters or application-neutral formats such as portable document format (PDF), project management repository should be employed to make access as transparent as possible. This leads to increased idea generation, new product ideas, and organizational learning from experiences. This repository will have individual and important components, such as:
>
> *Project Proposals*—previously used proposals, formats, templates, checklists, diagrams, and guidelines. Use and reuse is the intention, leading toward faster proposal delivery and decision making.
>
> *Project Plans*—previous project plans, possibly going back several years, of all project types, including many different plan types, such as quality, risk assessment, communication, implementation plans, etc. A valuable factor in project plans will be getting access to project resource estimates.
>
> *File Templates*—any useful templates used in managing projects, checklists, spreadsheets, and presentations.
>
> *Resources*—details of available project resources, both internal and external, with links to the Internet. These details include where the resources are located, availability, skill

Project Management and the Internet

▶ Introduction

Never before has there been a medium so profound that has had so much dramatic and rapid effect on our society, culture, and the way we conduct business. Not since the invention of electricity, flight, the wheel, and perhaps even gunpowder has there been such a technology that has been accepted so quickly. The Internet has seemed to spring almost from nowhere and burst upon society so quickly—all in a few short years. However, the Internet has been in existence since the early 1970s but only to the privileged few of the academic community. Probably over 90% of Internet users have come to use it in the past six years, since 1992, when the World Wide Web (WWW), a key Internet technology, became available. The Internet is much more than just the WWW. It has abundant resources in newsgroups and email. This wealth of resources and easy access through the Internet has particular benefits for project management.

The factors that have brought about the Internet phenomenon require some further analysis:

211

1. *The pursuit of global economy*—Corporations large and small, small businesses, and individuals are now required to seek new markets for goods and services in areas that they would not have considered perhaps 5 or even 10 years ago. The Internet is a means for achieving this objective by allowing anyone in any part of the world who has a computer and telephone to communicate with anyone else in the world and to conduct business.

2. *The powerful personal computer*—The PC has evolved in power, capacity, and speed as the cost has dropped. The Internet would be available only as a corporate and academic tool if the PC was not invented, and access to the Internet and its growth would be severely limited without the PC's capabilities. Imagine trying to access the Internet via a 3270-type device or green screen for any length of time.

3. *Falling communication costs*—Having cheap, fast communication is a very important part of the equation. Expect to see the costs continue to drop and access speeds continue to rise. The newer, faster, and improved Internet2 or the Next Generation Internet project that is proposed will be needed. Internet access speed is key to future success. We want to access information much more quickly—by a factor of at least 100.

4. *User demand*—When users demand a service, corporations and entrepreneurs supply it. Users want faster and cheaper access to information. The demand to see and experience other cultures, the pursuit of education, and the requirements for knowledge are also driving forces to Internet growth.

5. *Simpler software*—The increased development and widespread availability of good, high-quality software that everyone can use and use quickly to find information. Project managers can now search for ready-made project plans, recruit staff, increase communications, and create virtual project teams in time scales unimagined just a few years ago.

   The expansion and growth of the Internet will continue to change the face of computers and communications as we know it today. It promises universal access to anyone, anywhere, linking every computer to anyone who may want to use it.

   The Internet is not owned by any single entity, government, or commercial body. Therefore, it can evolve in ways that are market driven—what the people want they can now get. Add to this the constant media hype of new products, web pages,

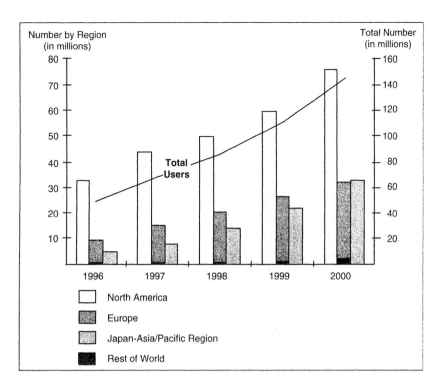

Figure 17–1   Growth of Internet Users. (*Source: Dataquest*)

software, and new net gadgets that feed the process. The number of people who will access it continues to grow, as shown in Figure 17–1.

6. *Content*—Information is continuously being added to the Internet at a rapid rate. Information not available today is readily available tomorrow, often in many forms. Conversely, information can disappear, change sites, hosts, or servers. Information can be deleted, changed, or restyled. One estimate puts the actual number of web pages at over 3 billion and growing rapidly.

7. *Format*—Information on the Internet is available in multiple formats. There are pure text files, graphics files, and everything else in between. There is no real standard for the Internet (some might argue that the Hypertext Markup Language [HTML] is the de facto standard, but this applies only to the WWW).

8. *Growth*—The Internet is very dynamic and has almost uncontrollable growth. Anyone who has access to a computer, even a small personal computer, a modem, and a telephone line can add information to the Internet. This means that it is very difficult to manage the size, growth, traffic, and many other technical resources required for such a complex network of computers. When the Internet started in 1969, it had just four computers. In 1974, five years later, there were 62. In 1984, there were 1,024. In 1990, there were 313,000. Today, the figure is over 38,000,000 (estimate only) and growing rapidly.

Some estimates put a new web page appearing every four seconds and tens of thousands of new users getting online every day. It took less than 5 years for the Internet to reach over 50 million users. When comparing that growth to other technologies, it startles the imagination. Cable television took 10 years to reach 50 million, regular television took 13 years, the telephone took 48 years. The truth is that no one knows for sure, and conclusive figures are difficult to verify.

▶ Personal Computers, Growth and the Internet

Table 17–1 is an analysis of the growth of personal computers by geographic region over time. What is particularly interesting in this table is the small percentage of personal computers that have access to the Internet at the present time—currently at only 26% of the total number out there. The question now arises, What happens if that percentage increases, and how will the Internet deal with this enormous volume? We will be faced with huge numbers of users in an already crowded and tangled web.

Table 17-1 Statistics of Worldwide Personal Computers

	1996	1997	1998	1999	2000
Europe	9,000,000	15,000,000	20,000,000	26,000,000	32,000,000
North America	32,000,000	43,500,000	50,000,000	60,000,000	75,000,000
Japan	4,000,000	7,000,000	11,000,000	17,000,000	24,000,000
Asia Pacific	500,000	1,000,000	2,000,000	4,000,000	9,000,000
Rest of World	200,000	500,000	1,000,000	2,000,000	3,000,000
Worldwide	45,700,000	67,000,000	84,000,000	109,000,000	143,000,000
Total PCs Worldwide	230,000,000	277,000,000	320,000,000	350,000,000	370,000,000
% of PCs on Internet	20%	24%	26%	31%	39%
Business at Business	30,000,000	42,000,000	50,000,000	64,000,000	89,000,000
SOHO[1]	2,200,000	3,000,000	4,000,000	6,000,000	7,000,000
Consumer	13,500,000	22,000,000	30,000,000	39,000,000	47,000,000
Total	45,700,000	67,000,000	84,000,000	109,000,000	143,000,000

1. SOHO—small office/home office

▶ Implications for Project Management

Having such a dynamic and powerful technology available in any corporation has profound implications for project management. Size, speed, availability, and access provide a powerful set of tools with which to make project management successful. However, it is not suggested that we eliminate the face-to-face contact that project teams need. However, by using the collaborative and communication tools of the Internet, we have the potential of leveraging technology for better project management. As we have learned, often by experiencing painful lessons, one key aspect we need to do more of in project management is *communicate*.

▶ The Virtual Office

Central to the future of the office and the workplace are fundamental changes in the nature of business. These changes and the impact of globalization, increasing competition, and the virtual enterprise are resulting in new work processes and environments, new models of organizational structure, and emerging "virtual corporations." We describe this as an entity that has little physical presence in bricks and mortar but enormous intellectual presence in terms of software and communications.

Virtual corporations are dependent on telecommunications to enable project management among dispersed staffers. Early virtual companies relied on limited e-mail applications, telephone systems, and fax, and were less than successful. More flexible and extensive movement toward virtualization demands more complete support of worker interaction and work processes for dispersed workers across traditional enterprise boundaries.

These factors produce fundamental change in the nature of work. The traditional office as the workplace will become greatly obsolete in time. In its place is emerging a model for an electronic workplace and a foundation built on Internet standards and intranets.

Making this approach a reality depends on an executive management perspective that the ability of the enterprise to transact business, sustain mission-critical processes, which are increasingly digital in nature, and support the highly dispersed nature of the work force with appropriate facilities requires an enterprise electronic workplace.

The monumental forces at work that are driving massive and profound changes in the technologies, architectures, implementation models, and management approaches of virtually every business have been described above. These forces are reshaping the workplace environment, recasting the technology used to support and fuel it, and redefining the role of technology for project workers and knowledge workers in particular.

An Internet Project Management Model

Clearly, the Internet and its associated technologies can be used as a powerful tool in project management. The following list provides examples of how an Internet Project Management (I-PM) model can be created:

- Provide an automated means of capturing, organizing, and maintaining project management content
- Optimize the use of existing technology (e.g., intranets, e-mail, and groupware)
- Support and expand technology with existing staff
- Develop recruitment practices using the Internet
- Conduct pilot project management projects; earn early visible results
- Select technology that is easy to replicate and for which it is easy to build skills, training, implementation, standards
- Provide a user-centric interface (intuitive, point-and-click, minimal training required)
- Minimize requirements for specialized project management software
- Enable electronic collaboration, feedback, and quality process improvement
- Manage disparate forms of content (e.g., files, text, video, and graphics)
- Support "push and pull" technologies

Communication

Specifically, let's examine the detailed benefits of the Internet that are valuable for increasing project management communication in such areas as:

- Communicating with users, management, vendors
- Getting agreement on designs, specifications, business case
- Documenting formal project meetings, actions, issues, task lists

- Recruiting for permanent and contract staff (see below)
- Application development
  - Creating and distributing system, program specs
  - Checking new code, finding routines
  - Verifying models, diagrams, charts
  - Generating test results, test data
  - Communicating progress, project plans
  - Resolving quality reviews and content
  - Tracking budgets and project date, milestones, deliverables

Discussion centers or, to use its Internet equivalent, chat rooms, can be beneficial. A Project Management Communications Center provides online chat rooms, threaded discussion rooms, and a facility to subscribe to and participate in internal or external e-mail distribution lists. Project members can solve problems, get advice and referrals for software, and exchange project plans, text documents, templates, presentations, and much more.

▶ Recruitment

The Internet is a fertile ground for recruiting for corporations looking for new staff for project teams. Project managers and human resource departments can locate needed staff from vast pools on the Internet. Huge web sites are now available to post resumes and match personal requirements such as location, salary, and technical skills. These web sites operate on a national, regional, state, and local basis. There are now thousands of positions available to choose from. This opens up an entirely new range of possibilities for the recruiter at the other end of the telephone. Some sites have software agents that match requirements to positions and send opportunity notices daily through e-mail. Corporations with a web presence almost always have a careers or jobs section on their web sites, and this is proving to be a valuable tool in the recruitment process.

One possible downside to the Internet as a recruitment tool is that project staff will be tempted to move around to better opportunities more often. One way to avoid this is with a good staff retention plan.

The better the benefits offered, the more likely it will be that staff will stay with projects (see Chapter 4).

Some sites, e.g., Yahoo (see *http://www.yahoo.com*) and many others offer huge directories just for recruitment. A small sample follows.

- Dice (*www.dice.com*)—A web recruiting site that is primarily focused on technical recruiting.
- The Job Connection (*www.jobconnection.com*)—A site comprised of many employment recruiting firms that operate on a national, regional, state, and local basis.
- Jobmall (*www.jobmall.co.uk*)—A site at which you may search for job vacancies or browse the arcades of recruitment agencies.
- Jobs jobs jobs (*www.jobserve.com/jjj*)—A guide to UK recruitment web sites.
- Monster (*www.monster.com*)—A site that provides a huge repository of positions and candidate resumes, as well as intelligent agents to speed up searching and notification of available positions that match criteria.
- Recruiters Online Network (*www.recruitersonline.com*)—A worldwide online association and resource for industry professionals.
- 4Work (*www.4work.com*)—A job listings and subscription-based job search agent.
- Job Bank (*www.jobbankusa.com*)—U.S. employment and resume information services for job candidates, employers, and recruitment firms. Job metasearch feature accesses large Internet employment databases.
- Techies.com (*www.techies.com*)—A site dedicated to recruiting of technical professionals.

To illustrate the potential for recruiting, this author conducted an experiment while writing this book. I posted my resume on one site to gauge the reaction. This site reports the number of times that your file is accessed. My resume was accessed 108 times over a two-week period.

The Internet is valuable for finding very specific, short-term contractor or consulting skills needed in a project. For example, let's say that we need a Novell network administrator, with Windows NT and Cisco

Routing Prerelease Management experience, but we need this person for only three months. By advertising on the Internet, there is a very good chance that the skills will be found. Candidates can be invited to send resumes, fees, and availability by e-mail to the appropriate project manager.

▶ Training

The Internet is playing an invaluable role in training in two specific areas:

1. Announcements, new information on certification, standards, courses, seminars, as well as enrolling in vendor courses.
2. Taking courses via the Internet or distance learning. Many virtual training organizations exist to allow remote students or employees to be continually up to date on the latest techniques.

▶ Conclusions

The Internet will begin to play an increasing and dynamic role in all project management activities. At present, like many Internet applications, project management via the Internet is still in its infancy. Expect to see dynamic growth in the next five years as software vendors ply their wares in the marketplace and success stories circulate. Senior management or CIOs will implement any technology that makes them more successful, and the business case for Internet use is sound in terms of value and return on investment.

As Christopher Meyer says in his excellent book, *Fast Cycle Time*:

> *The competitor who consistently, reliably, and profitably provides the greatest value to the customer first, wins. There are no other rules.*

The infrastructure of the Internet is in place, the access is available to anyone, it is cheap and ubiquitous as the telephone, and project management can only benefit.

Software Engineering Institute

▶ Introduction

In 1984, the U.S. Department of Defense set up funding for a software research and development center known as the Software Engineering Institute (SEI). A competitive bid contract was issued in December of that year and, after evaluation, was awarded to Carnegie Mellon University in Pennsylvania. Since then, technical and administrative professionals from industry, government, and academia have staffed it, providing products and services to industry and commerce, as well as to government.

The SEI embarked on a strategy to bring an engineering-type discipline to the development and evolution of software and to prepare individual professionals and organizations to improve their practices. For example, probably its most noted success has been the Capability Maturity Model (CMM®) Software that organizations use as a basis for appraisal and subsequent incremental process improvement. The objective is to help organizations achieve sufficient maturity to manage technology introduction. This strategy enabled development of an infrastructure into which technology and the means to establish priorities may be installed.

▶ Mission and Charter

The U.S. Department of Defense established the SEI to advance the practice of software engineering because quality software that is produced on schedule and within budget is a critical component of U.S. defense systems. Its mission is:

> To provide leadership in advancing the state of the practice of software engineering to improve the quality of systems that depend on software.

The SEI accomplishes this mission by promoting the evolution of software engineering from an ad-hoc, labor-intensive activity to a formal and professional discipline that is well managed and supported by technology, people, and practices.

The SEI charter is to:

1. Bring the ablest professional minds and the most effective technology to bear on the rapid improvement of the quality of operational software in systems that depend on software.
2. Accelerate the reduction to practice of modern software engineering techniques and methods.
3. Promulgate the use of modern techniques and methods throughout the defense community.

▶ Products and Services

The SEI has developed a wide portfolio of products and services that it offers for sale to any organization interested. These can be divided into a number of categories:

- **Engineering Practices**—SEI staff consults with numerous organizations to improve software architectures, systems security, and commercial off-the-shelf software (COTS), as well as other types of software.
- **Technology Adoption**—SEI staff provide services related to technology development and transition, measurement and analysis, and team-based processes.

- **Management Practices**—The SEI works to improve IT management practices, software acquisition, project management process improvements, and more.
- **Conferences and Courses**—Each year, the staff at SEI conduct public seminars, conferences, workshops, and events at centers throughout the United States.
- **Publications**—A series of technical reports, handbooks, papers, and advice is available either on-line via SEI's website or in hard copy.
- **Collaboration**—The SEI actively promotes collaborative ventures and advisory boards with industry and commerce to improve software development management practices.

▶ Author's Recommendation

Every organization involved with developing applications or software should review the prospect of implementing the CMM. It has been proven to provide significant process improvements in all areas of management and project management. It has enhanced the basic model to include People Capability Maturity Model (P-CMM) and the Software Acquisition Maturity Model (S-CMM). We can expect further developments and future models in the coming years.

▶ Conclusion

The SEI has established itself over a long period of time as the premier organization for software, process, and management improvement in the United States. Regrettably for the rest of the world, it does not provide anything outside of the continental United States. That is a great pity because much could be transferred to countries eagerly waiting to improve their management practices.

The SEI is best known for CMM, which is fast becoming the de facto standard for maturity process improvement. It provides a scalable model to improve over time. The model is being used by thousands of organizations in the United States.

For more information, contact:

Customer Relations
Software Engineering Institute
Carnegie Mellon University
Pittsburgh, PA 15213-3890
Phone, Voice Mail, and On-Demand FAX: (412) 268-5800
E-mail: *customer-relations@sei.cmu.edu*

Or visit its website at *www.sei.cmu.edu*

Project Management Institute

▶ Introduction

Since its founding in 1969 and now past its thirtieth anniversary year, the Project Management Institute (PMI) has grown to be an organization for the development of project management professionalism. With almost 65,000 members worldwide, the PMI is a nonprofit professional association. It promotes project management standards, provides seminars and informative programs, and professional certification for individuals within organizations.

Its stated organizational purpose is:

> *The Project Management Institute is an international organization working to improve project and program performance by serving its members, the profession, society, and a wide range of publics, application areas, and cultures.*

As part of this purpose, its corresponding guiding principles are as follows:

- PMI shall strive for effective communication, cooperation, and collaboration.

- PMI shall conduct its business in a fair manner.
- PMI shall be accountable to its members to advance the profession.
- PMI shall provide quality products and programs.
- PMI shall be member driven and shall address selected needs responsibly and honestly.

▶ Certification

Among the most valuable programs offered by the PMI is its certification program in project management. PMI's Project Management Professional (PMP) credential is increasingly becoming the recognized certification credential for the project management profession. To obtain PMP certification, an individual must satisfy educational and experience requirements, agree and adhere to a Code of Ethics, and pass the PMP Certification Examination. Worldwide, there are over 12,000 PMPs who provide project management services in 26 countries.

▶ International Awards

PMI's annual International Awards Program recognizes outstanding performance in the practice of project management and the contributions of individuals to the project management profession and to the Institute.

PMI's International Project of the Year is awarded to a project passing a rigorous three-tier selection process whose team members have superior performance in the application of project management principles and techniques. In 1998, this award went to the National Aeronautics and Space Administration's (NASA) Mars Pathfinder project. The Mars Pathfinder project was the second mission launched under the Discovery Program initiative for small planetary missions. It was designed as an engineering demonstration of key technologies and concepts for use in future missions to Mars.

Additionally, PMI honors individuals who have made sustained and significant contributions to the project management profession through both research and development, and for outstanding service to the project management profession or to PMI itself. Still other awards acknowledge the outstanding contributions of volunteers at the Institute's Chapter and Special Interest Group (SIG) levels.

▶ Seminars and Education

The PMI provides a continuing series of seminars in major cities of the United States as well as London, England and, soon, in other European cities. Educational seminars prepare individuals for the PMPC. A variety of offerings provides members with elementary and basic topics on practical and advanced management subjects. Seminars are also sponsored for specific industry types, such as finance, banking, and manufacturing. PMI is an authorized sponsor member of the International Association for Continuing Education and Training.

Among the list of topics and subjects are the following:

- Earned Value Application Fundamentals
- Effective Estimating on Projects
- Building and Leading High-Performance Teams
- A Focus on the Project Management Controlling Processes
- How to Capture Customer Requirements and Develop Project Scope
- Project Management: The Fundamentals
- Leadership, Power, Influence, Politics, and Negotiations
- Leading Complex Projects
- Life after Closeout: Managing Your Work and Career
- Managing at a Distance: Successful Management of Distributed Projects
- Managing Multiple Projects
- Managing Risk on Projects
- Mastering Contracts for Project Management
- Influencing without Authority
- Project Management Basic Skills

- Project Management for the Experienced Professional
- Project Management in a Global Environment
- The Project Office: Adding Value and Producing Results
- Project Planning and Control Toolbox
- Rapid Product Development
- Satisfying Stakeholders through Superior Quality

▶ Recruitment

The PMI provides a worldwide recruitment service for both employers and people seeking project management positions.

▶ Membership Offerings

Membership is open to anyone who is interested in advancing the profession of project management, and three categories are currently offered:

1. Student Membership
2. Individual Membership
3. Corporate Membership

▶ Recommendation

PMI is the author of a 200-page report called *A Guide to the Project Management Body of Knowledge*. Although it was last updated in 1996, it is still a valuable document to read and digest. It has many examples of diagrams and matrices used in project management. Further, it has what this author considers to be one of the best glossaries on project management terms and acronyms found anywhere in the world. The report can be downloaded free from its web site at: *www.pmi.org*

▶ More Information

Contact the PMI at its main location:

Project Management Institute Headquarters
Four Campus Boulevard
Newtown Square, Pennsylvania 19073-3299 USA
Phone: (610) 356-4600
Fax: (610) 356-4647
E-Mail: *pmihq@pmi.org*

Or visit its web site at *www.pmi.org*

Additional Project Management Resources

▶ Center for International Project and Program Management

The Center for International Project and Program Management (CIPPM) is an international association and center of advanced communication, research, and learning for professional project managers and those interested in project management. CIPPM exists to serve, support, and advance project and quality management, which serves society, including public and private business, politics, and the general public. Founded in 1987, CIPPM is a nonprofit organization based in Ann Arbor, Michigan at the University of Michigan, currently serving 6,900 members and affiliates. CIPPM sponsors events internationally.

For more information on the CIPPM, see its web site at *www.iol.ie/~mattewar/CIPPM*

▶ Guide to Project Management Web Sites

This site, based in Sweden, has many links to educational and commercial organizations that are doing research work into project management. If you're looking for educational research materials, this is a good place to start. See the web site at *www.hh.umu.se/fek/irnop/projweb.html*

▶ International Journal of Project Management

This is an international journal on project management, and it also has a web site. The table of contents of past issues is a starting point. See the web site at *www.elsevier.nl:80/locate/issn/02637863*

▶ THE INTERNATIONAL RESEARCH NETWORK

The International Research Network on Organizing by Projects is a center for information on organizations that are working on or researching themselves by project. There is a number of links here to sites in Europe and a number of references to printed materials. See the web site at *www.fek.umu.se/irnop/*

▶ Project Management Institute of Canada

PMI Canada is the Canadian association of project managers. This group is affiliated with the Project Management Institute (PMI) in the United States. See its web site at *www.pmicanada.com*

The Program/Project Management Initiative

The Program/Project Management Initiative (PPMI) web site provides NASA managers with agency-wide training information and project management tools. Features include a discussion group area, daily tips, readings, and a lexicon of NASA terms. A rich resource of NASA project management data, techniques, and information can be found at *http://www.hq.nasa.gov/office/HR-Education/training/ppmi.htm*

The Project Manager's Reference Site

The Project Manager's Reference Site is a UK-based site that provides a range of information for project managers. The site is largely Microsoft Project-oriented but includes information and links to many other commercial products and services. Recommended. See the web site at *http://www.projectmanagement.com*

The Project Management Forum

The Project Management Forum is a nonprofit resource for information on international project management affairs dedicated to development, cooperation, promotion, and support of a professional and worldwide project management discipline. Contact them at *www.pmforum.org/warindex.htm*

U.S. Army Corps of Engineers

The United States Army Corps of Engineers project management AIS and associated reports provide valuable information with links to other military corps systems. Its address is:

U.S. Army Corps of Engineers
Washington DC, 20314-1000 USA
Phone: (202) 761-8594

Fax: (202) 761-5295

Website: *www.usace.army.mil/inet/functions/cw/cecwb/pro-mis/promisx.htm*

▶ The International Project Management Help Desk

The International Project Management Help Desk (IPMHD) was founded to provide assistance to the international project management community and to promote project management fundamentals. It has numerous links to sites and additional resources for project managers. See its web site at *www.geocities.com/Athens/Delphi/8390*

▶ Association for Project Management

The Association for Project Management (APM) exists to help its members and to advance and promote the profession of project management, its skills and practice. It is the only UK-based organization dedicated to advancing the science of project management and the professional development of project managers and project management specialists. Its web site is: *www.synapse.net/~loday/PMForum/apm.htm*

▶ ProjectNet

The ProjectNet project management resource site is managed by *Project Manager Today*, the UK's project management monthly magazine. Its web site is *www.projectnet.co.uk*

▶ Professional and Standards Organizations

International Project Management Association	IPMA is the recognized international nonprofit network type of organization for qualified project management. IPMA's vision is to be the prime promoter of project management as a powerful tool for management of change. IPMA started in 1965 as a discussion group of managers of international projects. The first international Congress was held in 1967 in Vienna, with participants from 30 different countries. Since that time, IPMA has developed steadily and is now the prime international promoter of project management in Europe, Asia, and Arabian countries. A most significant characteristic of IPMA is the parallel development of 18 associated national societies that serve the specific development needs of each country in its own language. IPMA has emerged as the representative body of an international network of national project management societies.
Association of Project Managers	The Association of Project Managers exists to help its members and to advance and promote the profession of project management, its skills and practice. It is a UK-based organization dedicated to advancing the science of project management and the professional development of project managers and project management specialists.
International Standards Organization	ISO comprises more than 180 technical committees, covering many industry sectors and products. The American Society for Quality Control (ASQC) administers the U.S. Technical Advisory Group (TAG), which presents its views to the international ISO technical committees. The U.S. TAG to ISO Technical Committee 176 consists of quality experts who work with the international committee to draft, revise, and word ISO 9000+ (10000) quality assurance and quality management documents.
American National Standards Institute	Founded in 1918, the American National Standards Institute (ANSI) is a private, not-for-profit membership organization that coordinates the U.S. voluntary consensus standards system and approves American National Standards. ANSI consists of approximately 1,300 national and international companies, 30 government agencies, 20 institutional members, and 250 professional, technical, trade, labor, and consumer organizations. ANSI acts to insure that a single consistent set of consensus-based American National Standards are developed by ANSI-accredited standards developers. Integral to the development and approval process is the requirement that all interests concerned have the opportunity to participate in the development process.

American Society for Quality Control

The American Society for Quality Control (ASQC) is the worldwide leader in the development, promotion, and application of quality and quality-related technologies for the quality profession, private sector, government, and academia. Its goal: To create a greater awareness of the need for quality, to promote research and the development of standards, and to provide educational opportunities to ensure product and service excellence through improved quality.

Founded in 1946 as a direct result of World War II efforts, ASQC's original purpose was to improve the quality of defense materials. Today, ASQC serves its 70,000 individual members and 650 corporate members through publications, courses, national and international conferences and seminars, professional certification programs, and local meetings and events conducted by its 210 sections, 15 divisions, and 9 technical committees.

A Sample Crisis Plan

An Outline of a Crisis Communications Plan—That Works

▶ Introduction

Most corporations, especially large companies, expect a crisis, but have no plans to deal with one. A recent crisis communications conference in Washington DC revealed that 95% of CEOs fully anticipate an eventual crisis at their companies, and yet less than half have a plan to respond. Of those who do have crisis plans, many are unwieldy, unrealistic, or out of date.

1. **Immediately train in media communications,** that is, talking to the press, TV, and other media, a project manager for at least one key executive. Video-feedback coaching for one management-level person, at minimum. That would give one person who knows how to work with the press constructively. Two coached executives would be better, with one available when the other is not. Project Management—always have a back-up.

2. **Establish a crisis team.** This team manages the crisis while the rest of the staff runs the company. A workable team contains three to six people. Good teams for larger companies involve the Chief Operating Officer, the General Counsel, and the Corporate Communications Officer. Assign these team members to crises for which they are best suited. For example, consider the COO for policy or financial problems, the General Counsel for legal, and the Communications Officer for physical disasters. Each team member should then identify other resource people to assist them. Choose these resource people for their knowledge and judgment, not their rank. All involved, or their alternates, should be reachable seven days a week. During a crisis, consider letting the CEO do what he or she knows best, leading the company. That makes the next step vital.

3. **Pre-authorize the crisis team.** The CEO should endorse the team and the plan in advance. This gives a green light to the fast action so critical in containing emergencies. They have to make important decisions and they will need the authority to proceed. Indecision is one of the worst enemies in a crisis.

4. **Designate spokesperson(s) and media coach them.** Identify the best overall spokesperson. If necessary, identify different spokespersons for different crises. If the corporation has headquarters with branches in other cities, consider having qualified spokespeople at the branches. In tough times, citizens prefer to hear from people they know, rather than from distant corporate officers speaking through news releases. Media coach all of them.

5. **Establish valuable communications principles.** These are your goals for what you want to communicate to your various audiences. Some good crisis principles, in priority order, are: A) Take care of those most effected (victims) first, B) Brief employees, C) Brief the press, D) Reassure all audiences that you are acting in their best interest, E) Remain open and accessible, F) Provide information as fast as possible, and G) Keep no secrets from the public. Good communications principles compel you to say and do the right thing.

6. **Establish media notification procedures.** List all media contacts wherever you do business, including names, titles, phone, and fax numbers. Keep the lists current. You want to be able to reach them within minutes.

BORDERS

BORDERS
BOOKS MUSIC AND CAFE
100 Broadway
New York, NY 10005
(212)964-1988

STORE: 0566   REG: 03/91 TRAN#: 8918
SALE   12/12/2006 CHR: 00221

PROJECT MGMT
        6381259   SC T   31.49
  44.99 30% WITH COUPON
COUPON 15901438000000000004
CHINESE LANGUAGE MAP
        6456879   MP T   7.85
CD CHINESE LEVEL 1 & 2
        7933924   DR T   197.40
329.00 40% WITH COUPON
COUPON 15901791000000000000

              Subtotal   236.84
BR: 8373872947   S 10%   23.69-

              Subtotal   213.15
HOLIDAY SAVINGS REWARDS   3.28-

              Subtotal   209.87
              NY 8.375%   17.58
  3 Items   Total   227.45
            MASTERCARD   227.45
ACCT # /S XXXXXXXXXXXX6897
              AUTH: 027908
NAME: SNYDER/ANDREW

          CUSTOMER COPY

You Saved $172.07

       12/12/2006 06:29PM

BORDERS.

Returns to Borders Stores

Merchandise presented for return, including sale or marked-down items, must be accompanied by the original Borders store receipt or a Borders Gift Receipt. Returns must be completed within 30 days of purchase. For returns accompanied by a Borders Store Receipt, the purchase price will be refunded in the medium of purchase (cash, credit card or gift card). Items purchased by check may be returned for cash after 10 business days. For returns within 30 days of purchase accompanied by a Borders Gift Receipt, the purchase price (after applicable discounts) will be refunded via a gift card.

Merchandise unaccompanied by the original Borders store receipt, Borders Gift Receipt, or presented for return beyond 30 days from date of purchase, must be carried by Borders at the time of the return. The lowest price offered for the item during the 6 month period prior to the return will be refunded via a gift card.

Opened videos, music discs, cassettes, electronics, and audio books may only be exchanged for a replacement of the original item.

Periodicals, newspapers, out-of-print, collectible, pre-owned items, and gift cards may not be returned.

Returned merchandise must be in saleable condition.

BORDERS.

Returns to Borders Stores

Merchandise presented for return, including sale or marked-down items, must be accompanied by the original Borders store receipt or a Borders Gift Receipt. Returns must be completed within 30 days of purchase. For returns accompanied by a Borders Store Receipt, the purchase price will be refunded in the medium of purchase (cash, credit card or gift card). Items purchased by check may be returned for cash after 10 business days. For returns within 30 days of purchase accompanied by a Borders Gift Receipt, the purchase price (after applicable discounts) will be refunded via a gift card.

Merchandise unaccompanied by the original Borders store receipt, Borders Gift Receipt, or presented for return beyond 30 days from date of purchase, must be carried by Borders at the time of the return. The lowest price offered for the item during the 6 month period prior to the return will be refunded via a gift card.

Opened videos, music discs, cassettes, electronics, and audio books may only be exchanged for a replacement of the original item.

Periodicals, newspapers, out-of-print, collectible, pre-owned items, and gift cards may not be returned.

7. **Conduct a vulnerability audit.** This is a centerpiece effort. Interview top managers and survey supervisors to catalog potential crises. Critique existing plans, if any, to deal with them. Discuss past crises and what happened, lessons learned. Prioritize your vulnerabilities and how to react to them.

8. **Establish internal/external communications mechanisms.** Formulate phone trees from contacting all company personnel, clients, stockholders, authorities, and emergency personnel. Larger companies should establish and outfit crisis command centers, media briefing centers, and know how to create rumor control hotlines.

9. **Media coach all spokespeople and officials who deal with the media.** Once the crisis plan is in place, everyone should have a certain comfort level with talking to reporters under both normal and emergency situations.

10. **Meet quarterly, drill annually, review biennially.** A crisis plan should be a living, breathing, workable document. Seasonal meetings, yearly drills, and periodic plan reviews will keep it current. It pays to manage a crisis—or else you might not recover from it, and crises happen at unexpected times.

Index

requirements specification, 94
system interfaces, designing, 92
technical design, 90–92
tools, 96–97
user documentation outline, 95
workflow diagram, 95
design reports and documents, 90
design screens, 89
design sign-off, 96
design work units, 101
designer roles, 103
detailed design, 100–102
detailed results, checking, 114–115
development alternatives, evaluating, 73

E

end user documentation, 133
end user interface design, 89–90, 95
end user requirements
analyzing system requirements, 82
current design, recovering, 81
data model, creating, 84
event model, creating, 84
identifying, 81
metrics and goals, establishing, 82
overview, 80–81
prototype business process, 82–84
quality requirements, 81–82
work flow and organization, confirming, 81
enhancements, documenting potential, 132
enterprise model, 86
event model, creating, 84
executive sponsor role, 74

F

follow-on potential, 41
functional completeness, verifying, 92

G

Gantt charts, 6–7
Gantt, Henry, 6–7
Guide to Project Management Web Sites, 232

H

hardware environment, identifying, 72
Hierarchy of Needs Model (Maslow), 49–50
human factors specialist role, 85, 120

I

Implementation Planning Phase, 60

Industrial Revolution, 4–5
information plan, 75, 86
insecurity of IT staff, reasons for, 49–50
integration test, performing, 114
International Journal of Project Management, 232
International Project Management Association, 235
International Project Management Help Desk (IPMHD), 234
International Research Network, 232
International Standards Organization, 235
Internet
as recruitment tool, 218–220
communication, 217–218
communication costs, 212
content, 213
format, 213
global economy, 212
growth, 214
implications for project management, 215
Internet Project Management (I-PM) model, 217
overview, 211–214
personal computers, 212, 214–215
software, 212–213
training, role in, 220
user demand, 212
virtual office, 216
interpersonal skills, 23

K

KM
benefits of, 208–209
best project management practices repository, 209
case studies, 207
file templates, 208
need for, 205–206
overview, 203–205
project management repository, 208
project plans, 208
project proposals, 208
resources, 208–209
sources of knowledge capital, 206–207
tools, 209
knowledge management. *See* KM
Kroger Company, 143–145

L

lifecycle

project staffing performance, 37
project standards, 29–31
project teams
    cost of IT staff replacement, 47–48
    demand for IT staff, 44–47
    insecurity of IT staff, reasons for, 49–50
    needs, meeting, 48–52
    replacement of IT staff, cost of, 47–48
    retention of IT staff, need for, 44–47
    retention packages, 50–52
    shortages in information technology staff, 43–44
    technology project staffing model, 46
project work plan, finalizing, 73–74
ProjectNet, 234
promotion process, 114
prototype business process, 82–84

Q

quality attributes, verifying, 93
quality checkpoints, 65
quality requirements, 87
quality reviews, 196–197
quality verification and validation, 92–93

R

RAD
    application complexity, 153
    benefits, 149
    concepts of, 148
    end users, 151–152
    existing architecture and technology, use of, 152
    improvements in productivity and speed, 159–160
    information specialists, 156–157
    Internet and, 153–154
    lifecycle, 149–150
    management sponsor, 155–156
    methodology, 152
    objectives, 149
    observers, 158–159
    overview, 147–148
    project management, 150–154
    RAD facilitator, 154–155
    scribe, 157–158
    specialists, 158
    team members, motivation of, 153
    team members, role of, 154–159
    time frame for development, 151
Rapid Application Development. *See* RAD

Rapid Application Development (Martin), 148
readiness check, performing, 131
receiving team, 66
release management, 193
release number, 64
replacement of IT staff, cost of, 47–48
requirements management, 190–191
requirements sign-off, 87
requirements specification, 86–87, 94
responsibilities, 62
retention of IT staff, need for, 44–47
retention packages, 50–52
reviewing present status, 71
revision process, 62–63
risk management
    assessing risks, 169
    Barings Bank and lack of, 162
    contingency, 171
    cost risks, 164
    enterprise risk profile, 171–172
    external risks, 163–164
    identifying risks, 167–169
    lack of, results when there is a, 162
    monitoring risks, 169
    objectives, 163
    operational risks, 165
    overview, 161
    plan for, 166–171
    process of, 166
    risk watch list, 169
    schedule risks, 164
    technology risks, 165
    types of risk, 163–165
Rollout Phase
    activities, 131–132
    change requests, 133
    conversion plan, 132
    conversion team, 132
    end user documentation, 133
    enhancements, documenting potential, 132
    inputs, 132–133
    milestones, 134
    objectives, 131
    operations instructions, 133
    outputs, 133
    postconversion review documents, 133
    postconversion review sign-off, 134
    production, monitoring, 132
    project management role, 132
    purpose, 130–131